Christianity

Made

Simple

(or Everything You Ever Wanted to Know About Being a Christian and Didn't Know How to Ask)

Suzanne Bower

Wendy
So great to have met you
Isaiah 53
Suzanne

Scripture references are taken from King James Version and the following:

NIV - New International Version] Holy Bible, New International Version ®. Copyright © 1973, 1978, 1984 International Bible Society, Zondervan

NKJV - New King James Version] ©1982, Thomas Nelson, Inc.

JPS – Jewish Publication Society Old Testament © 1917 public domain

Hebrew and Greek text, pronunciation, and definitions taken from Strong's Exhaustive Concordance of the Bible, by James Strong, S.T.D.,LL.D., Hendrickson Publishers

Editor's note: All underlined and bolded type on Scripture references is author's emphasis.

Available: www.createspace.com/3338335

Dedication

I dedicate this book with love to my daughter, Heather, my son, Isaac, my grandson, Benjamin and my great-granddaughter, Piper.

Table of Contents

Introduction

You are about to embark on the most exciting journey of your life. Jesus said:

"No man can come to me, except the Father which has sent me draw him..." (John 6:44)

It is no accident you picked up this book. The Father is drawing you into a relationship with Him and the only way into an intimate relationship with Him is through His son Jesus Christ. Jesus also said:

"I am the way, the truth, and the life: no one cometh unto the Father, except by me." (John 14:6)

If you desire to have an intimate, thrilling and powerful relationship with the Creator of the Universe who loves you as if you were His only child, who will care for you tenderly, meticulously and lovingly, meet all your needs and give you the desires of your heart, read on.

Foreword

My son once referred to me in an English term paper as a "wondering Christian". "No", he was quick to point out, "it is not 'wandering'. She is always wandering from church to church 'wondering' if she is missing anything". What I have observed in my wandering is that each denomination, or doctrinally affiliated group, has a strong understanding and emphasis of one or more aspects of Christianity, but no one group seems to have it all. At least, this is the way it has appeared to me.

One group was strong on helping people to come into a saving relationship with Christ, water baptism, and loving fellowship. Another group was grounded in communion and accepting people where they are while at the same time guiding and encouraging and instructing in how to live a holy life. Another group ministered the Baptism in the Holy Spirit, operated in the gifts of the Spirit and offered anointed teaching in these areas. Yet, another group was knowledgeable in the Word of Faith and offered anointed teaching and counseling on applying the Word to life in order to appropriate the blessings of God. Some taught on covenant and some taught on end-time prophecy. But, I have never encountered any one group who taught extensively on all these topics. This is not to say that they don't, I have just never received teaching in all these areas in any one church.

This led me to the desire to write this book. I am writing the kind of book I would like to have found when I first began seeking the Lord. I am not claiming to be an expert in all these areas, or indeed, in any of them. I am just hoping to share some of the wisdom I have gained in thirty years of diligently seeking God face-to-face in prayer, reading the Word from cover to cover continuously, and drinking in any teaching I have been privileged to have opportunity to either hear or read, in order "that I might know Him, and the power of His resurrection". (Philippians 3:10) I do not ask that you take my word as final in any area. Seek the Lord, and He will guide you. There are myriad studies available in all these areas. I am hoping this book will serve as an introduction to Jesus and what He has appropriated for us by His atoning sacrificial death on the cross.

What I am hoping to accomplish is that a person who has never been to church and isn't really sure which church to attend should they start, but has come to the place where they are seeking the truth about God - Who He is and What He is about - will pick up this book and at least find enough answers to bring them further along the way in their journey to Him. My greatest desire is that you would find Jesus in the pages of this book, fall in love with Him and want to spend the rest of your life serving Him and enjoying Him. He is worth it.

What is a Christian?

Through the centuries since Jesus Christ came, many things have been done in the name of Christianity which sometimes seem to be "un-Christian", to say the least. Furthermore, there are many different denominations of professing Christians with many diverse doctrines dividing them. That being the case it is no wonder we have so many differing views on what it means to be a Christian.

Webster's Online Dictionary defines a Christian as "A religious person who believes Jesus is the Christ and is a member of a Christian denomination".

To begin with, Christianity is not a "religion" *per se*. Religion is defined as "a system of attitudes, beliefs, and practices related to the supernatural". To be a Christian is far more than just having a "system of attitudes, beliefs and practices". It is to have a living, vital, breathing relationship with God Himself, as we will see as we go on. Religions impose rules for living whereby one can "merit" the favor of God. Christianity is a gift, purchased for us by the Blood of Christ, which bestows on us the totally unmerited favor of God freely and extravagantly poured out upon any who will simply receive by faith.

What does it mean to believe that Jesus is the Christ? The word Christ is translated from the Greek word *khris-tos'* which was translated from the Hebrew word *ma-shi'-ach* which means "anointed". Anointing symbolizes the presence of God. To believe that Jesus is the Christ means that He is the Presence of God among us. Another Name the Bible gives to Jesus is "Emmanuel". (Isaiah 7:14, Matthew 1:23) This is a Hebrew word *emanuel* meaning "God with us". Jesus is God coming to earth as a Man to dwell with us. The Bible tells us that when Mary conceived Jesus she was a virgin. An angel appeared to her and told her she would bear a child. She asked how could this be since she had never "known" (had intimate relations with) a man, and the angel told her the Holy Spirit (Who is God Himself) would come upon her and cause the child to be conceived in her womb.

And in the sixth month the angel Gabriel was sent from God unto a city of Galilee, named Nazareth,
To a virgin espoused to a man whose name was Joseph, of the house of David; and the virgin's name was Mary...

And the angel said unto her, Fear not, Mary: for thou hast found favor with God.
And, behold, thou shalt conceive in thy womb, and bring forth a son, and shalt call his name JESUS [Hebrew: *Yeshua*, which means "redeemer", "savior", or literally "God saves"]...

Then said Mary unto the angel, How shall this be, seeing I know not a man?
And the angel answered and said unto her, The Holy Ghost shall come upon thee, and the power of the Highest shall overshadow thee: therefore also that holy thing which shall be born of thee shall be called the Son of God. (Luke 1:26-35)

So to we see that to believe that Jesus is the Christ is to believe that He is the Son of God.

But believing alone is not enough. The Bible tells us even the devils believe Jesus is the Christ.

And devils also came out of many, crying out, and saying, Thou art Christ the Son of God. And he rebuking them suffered them not to speak: for they knew that he was Christ. (Luke 4:40, 41)

So we see that just believing Jesus is the Christ is not enough. Furthermore, being a "member of a Christian denomination" doesn't really make you a Christian according to what Jesus Himself said. One Bible teacher has said, "Going to church doesn't make you a Christian any more than sitting in my garage makes me a car."

Let's look at what Jesus said. When Nicodemus (a ruler of the Jews at the time of Jesus) came to Jesus, Jesus told him,

"Verily, verily, [truly, truly] *I say unto you, except a man be born again, he cannot see the kingdom of God".* (John 3:3)

So, we see that to be a Christian, we need to be "born again". What does this mean?

Being born again, not of corruptible seed, but of incorruptible, by the word of God, which liveth and abideth for ever. (1 Peter 1:23)

This passage says we are born again by the "seed" of the Word of God. How does this occur?

In the beginning was the Word, and the Word was with God, and the Word was God.
And the Word was made flesh, and dwelt among us, (and we beheld his glory, the glory as of the only begotten of the Father,) full of grace and truth.
(John 1:1, 14)

We see from this passage that the Jesus and the Word of God are one. So the seed is the Word and the Word is Jesus.

This passage goes on to say:

But as many as received him, to them gave he power to become the sons of God, even to them that believe on his name:
Which were born, not of blood, nor of the will of the flesh, nor of the will of man, but of God. (John 1:12)

So the "seed" of the Word, which is also Jesus, is sown into our hearts. (Luke 8:5 – 15)

When we "receive" Jesus through the Word we have heard, in other words we receive what the Word says about Him, that He is the Son of God, that He has risen from the dead, and that reconciliation to God comes from Him, we are born again.

How do we receive?

We must first believe, but there is one other thing.

"If you shall confess with your mouth the Lord Jesus, and shall believe in your heart that God has raised him from the dead, you shall be saved. For with the heart man believes unto righteousness; and with the mouth confession is made unto salvation." (Romans 10:9)

Again, from Romans 10:9 we see that just to believe is not enough. We must also "confess" with our mouths. The Greek word *hom-ol-og-eh'-o* translated as "confess", means "to say the same thing". In other words, we must **say the same thing** as the Word does. We will see why this is so important later on when we discuss Faith and Angels.

So, first of all to become a Christian, we must believe that Jesus is the Christ, the Son of God, and then we need to "confess" our belief. How do we do this? We pray. We "confess" to God the Father in prayer that we believe that Jesus is His son, and that He died for our sins, and we ask Him to cause us to be "born again" by His spirit and come to live on the inside of us and help us to be what He created us to be.

How do we know He will do this? Well, Jesus said,

"If a man love me, he will keep my words: and my Father will love him, and we will come unto him, and <u>*make our abode with him.*</u>*"* (John 14:23)

To "make our abode with him" means to live with him.

Basically, we could translate it this way, *"If anyone loves me, he will remember what I say and do it, and my Father will love him, and we will come to him and*

17

live with him".

Furthermore, Jesus prayed this prayer in the garden before He gave himself up to be crucified.

"And the glory which thou gave me I have given them; that they may be one, even as we are one: I in them, and you in me, that they may be made perfect in one; and that the world may know that you have sent me, and have loved them, as you have loved me. "
(John 17:23)

Now we begin to get a glimpse of what it is all about. Jesus is praying here to the Father concerning all who would believe on Him "that they would be one, even as we are one" and that "the world may know that you have sent me and have loved them, as you have loved me" [paraphrased]. He is praying here that we would know that the Father loves us as He loved Jesus, His only begotten son, and the result of that love in us is to make us "one" as Jesus and the Father are one.

When we walk in that kind of love, we will not do things which are unloving and "un-Christian". People who know they are loved are, in turn, loving. It is unloved people who are unloving. And only the Father's love can truly satisfy us down deep on the inside of us where we live.

Jesus tells us that there are two commandments on which all the others depend. The first is:

Thou shalt love the Lord thy God with all thy heart, and with all thy soul, and with all thy mind.
(Matthew 22:37)

And the second:

And the second commandment is like the first:
Thou shalt love thy neighbor as thyself.
(Matthew 22:38, 39)

In order to love God, we must get to know Him, and in order to love our neighbor we must have the love of God residing on the inside of us. How do we do that? By being "born again" and allowing Him to take up residence on the inside of us by His Spirit.

Well, you say, I would like to do that but I am not sure that I really believe all this. The Bible has an answer to this dilemma also. God said to Moses:

"I call heaven and earth to record this day against you,
[that] I have set before you life and death, blessing and
cursing: therefore choose life, that both you and your
seed [your descendents] *may live."* (Deuteronomy 30:19)

We see here that faith is a **choice**. We must choose to believe. Once we make that choice, and mean it, the confidence will follow. And how do we "choose life"? Well, Jesus said,

"I am the resurrection, and the life: he that believes in
me, though he were dead, yet shall he live: And
whosoever lives and believes in me shall never die."
(John 11:25,26)

So, we see that to choose life is to choose Jesus.
But there is one other thing.

Jesus continually preached;

"Repent, for the kingdom of Heaven is at hand"
(Matthew 4:17)

What does this mean? The Greek word *met-an-o-eh'-o* translated as "repent" means to change ones mind and direction, to change the way one is going. So, we need to change our heart from following our own plan to following God's plan.

When we follow our own plans and inclinations they will be selfish and self-seeking. The sad truth is that we deceive ourselves into thinking that our motives are pure. But the Bible tells us otherwise.

The heart is deceitful above all things, and desperately wicked: who can know it? (Jeremiah 17:9)

It is only when we allow God to examine us and direct our paths that we can be assured of living a righteous life. The Bible tells us,

Trust in the LORD with all thine heart; and lean not unto thine own understanding.
In all thy ways acknowledge him, and he shall direct thy paths. (Proverbs 3:5,6)

Notice it says "lean not" to our own understanding, but in all our ways acknowledge God, and He will direct our paths. This tells us we won't always know the right way to go, but God will guide us in His ways, if we will trust Him and allow Him.

If you have decided to receive Christ into your heart, to make Him Lord of your life, and to change your direction from your way to His way of abundant blessing on earth and eternal life after this one, just pray the following prayer:

Father God, I choose to believe that Jesus is your son, that He was born of the Virgin Mary, and that he died for my sins, rose again, and ascended into Heaven, from where He will come again in Glory with all who believe in Him. I ask you to forgive my sins, recreate me and cause me to be "born again" and send your Holy Spirit to live on the inside of me to help me to be all that you created me to be. I purpose in my heart to allow Jesus to be the Lord of my life, from this day forward, and to live my life according to your will allowing you to direct my life with your perfect love. AMEN.

If you feel you are not yet ready to pray this prayer, just put a marker in this page and come back to it when you are ready and keep reading. It will all become clearer as you read on and God has all the time in the world.

If you prayed this prayer, you have just experienced the greatest miracle in the world, the miracle of the new birth. You are now a new creation.

Therefore if any man be in Christ, he is a new creature: Old things are passed away and all things have become new. (II Corinthians 5:17)

Take a few minutes right now to just thank Jesus for what He has done for you and spend a little time in His presence getting to know Him. Your life has changed direction. You will never be the same.

Thanks be to God for his unspeakable gift.
 (II Corinthians 9:15)

What is sin?

The concept of sin has been as misrepresented and misunderstood over the years as the concept of Christianity. Many have categorized sin and defined it in such a way that one begins to think that Christianity is merely a lot of dos and don'ts and that it would take a lot of time and study to keep them straight. This is a part of the truth, and there is a good reason for it, but in the light of the New Covenant, it is a somewhat distorted version of the truth.

The central issue here is not sin, but Holiness. God is Holy and we are called to be Holy once we are His. (Leviticus 20:7, I Peter 1:15,16) Sin is the opposite of Holiness. But we cannot in our own strength conform to His Holiness. The Bible tells us,

"All have sinned and fallen short of the Glory of God". (Romans 3:23)

When we are "born again" we come into an intimate union with a Holy God. He lives on the inside of us. We are the "temple of the Holy Spirit".

What? know ye not that your body is the temple of the Holy Ghost which is in you, which ye have of God, and ye are not your own? (I Corinthians 6:19)

Our redemption from Hell and death was bought with the precious price of the blood of Jesus. If we are truly His and honor and appreciate His atoning sacrifice for us, we will not desire to do anything that will grieve or shame Him.

To put it another way, the Greek word *ham-ar-tee'-ah* used in the New Testament for "sin" means "to miss the mark". So we see that sin is not a matter of doing this or that, or not doing this or that, it is a matter of "missing the mark" of conforming to the holiness of a holy God.

But you say no one can do this! And you are right. This is why Jesus came and died for us. The Bible tells us "the wages of sin is death". This is pretty serious. But God knew we could not walk perfectly in His holiness in our own strength, so He provided an atonement. The definition of the word "atonement" is a "covering for sin". In the Old Covenant, animals were sacrificed for sin on a regular basis. When the animals were offered on the altar, fire came down from Heaven and consumed the sacrifice.

Now when Solomon had made an end of praying, the fire came down from heaven, and consumed the burnt offering and the sacrifices; and the glory of the LORD filled the house. (II Chronicles 7:1)

But in the New Covenant, Jesus became the final sacrifice for sin. This is the reason He had to die. And this is the reason the fire no longer comes down from Heaven to accept any other sacrifice. When He said on the cross *"It is finished"* (John 19:30) He meant the price had been paid in full for our sins. He has become our atonement. But He has become much more than that. We read in the account of the last supper in the Gospel of Matthew,

And he took the cup, and gave thanks, and gave it to them, saying, Drink ye all of it. [All of you, drink from it] *For this is my blood of the new testament, which is shed for many for the remission of sins.*
(Matthew 26:27,28)

He uses the word "remission" *of* sins here. The Greek word *af'-es-is* means "pardon, deliverance, forgiveness, remission". This is a much stronger concept than "atonement" which is just a "covering" for sin. Remission means to totally do away with.

If you have a bill, which is remitted, and you attempt to pay that same bill some time later, they will tell you that debt no longer exists. It is the same with our sin through Jesus' death on the cross.

When we receive forgiveness for our sin through His shed blood, that sin no longer exists. It is as if it never happened. This is truly the good news, which is the literal meaning of "gospel". [The Greek word for "gospel", *yoo-ang-ghel'-ee-on* means, literally, "good message".]

Isaiah prophesied, speaking of Jesus' death on the cross,

"But he [was] wounded for our transgressions, [he was] bruised for our iniquities: the chastisement of our peace [was] upon him; and with his stripes we are healed." (Isaiah 53:5)

This scripture tells us that it is our sin for which Jesus paid the punishment. This is the reason He was beaten and bruised. He took our place and paid the penalty for our sin. The scripture also tells us concerning Christ,

For he [God] *hath made him* [Christ] *to be sin for us, who knew no sin; that we might be made the righteousness of God in him.* (II Corinthians 5:21)

Jesus became our substitute, our "scapegoat". This is the reason that when you prayed the prayer to ask Jesus to forgive your sins, you can have the confidence that they are forgiven. Jesus paid the price for them in full. And the Holy Spirit living on the inside of you will give you the power to live a holy life if you allow Him to lead you daily, moment to moment. But when you fall short - and we all do,

"...when we confess our sin God is faithful to forgive our sin and to cleanse us from all unrighteousness."
(I John 1:9)

God will forgive our sin and cleanse us from all unrighteousness, but we must choose holiness and righteousness.

Maybe you feel we should be a little more specific about what particular actions constitute sin.

In the Old Covenant, which was the covenant God made with Abraham and later confirmed with Moses, the new birth was not available, because Jesus had not yet come and died and risen again to make it available. So, God gave the commandments to Moses in order that the people would be continually reminded of His existence, and in order to teach them how to live, day by day. The Ten Commandments which were given to Moses on the mountain [and about which there seems to be such a storm of controversy these days] were as follows:

1. *You shall have no other gods before Me.*
2. *You shall not make for yourself an idol in the form of anything in heaven above or on the earth beneath or in the waters below. You shall not bow down to them or worship them;*
3. *You shall not misuse the name of the Lord your God, for the Lord will not hold anyone guiltless who misuses his name.*
4. *Observe the Sabbath day by keeping it holy, as the Lord your God has commanded you. Six days you shall labor and do all your work, but the seventh day is a Sabbath to the Lord your God. On it you shall not do any work,*
5. *"Honor your father and your mother, as the Lord your God has commanded you, so that you may live long and that it may go well with you in the land the Lord your God is giving you.*
6. *You shall not murder.*
7. *You shall not commit adultery.*
8. *You shall not steal.*
9. *You shall not give false testimony against your neighbor.*
10. *You shall not covet your neighbor's wife. You shall not set your desire on your neighbor's house or land, his manservant or maidservant, his ox or donkey, or anything that belongs to your neighbor.* (Deuteronomy 5:7 - 21 NIV)

By the way, there were far more than ten

commandments, but these were the first ten which were given to Moses on the mountain. If you read the book of Leviticus, you will find detailed laws pertaining to daily life.

But God told Israel by the Prophet Jeremiah,

"Behold, the days come, says the LORD, that I will make a new covenant with the house of Israel, and with the house of Judah: But this [shall be] the covenant that I will make with the house of Israel; After those days, says the LORD, I will put my law in their inward parts, and write it in their hearts; and will be their God, and they shall be my people." (Jeremiah 31:31,33)

He is saying here that in the new covenant His laws would be written in our hearts, rather than on stone as He originally gave the law in the old covenant. How can that be? Well, God Himself is living on the inside of us to direct us by His Holy Spirit in the way we should go.

Jesus said,

"Howbeit when he, the Spirit of truth, is come, he will guide you into all truth." (John 16:13)

Since the Holy Spirit came on the day of Pentecost (Acts 2:1-4) He has always been with us to tell us what to do and what not to do. We must learn to listen.

Does this mean that we do not have to keep the old laws? By no means! Jesus said,

"Think not that I am come to destroy the law, or the prophets: I am not come to destroy, but to fulfill." (Matthew 5:17)

Does this mean that we need to know all the laws in the Old Testament and live by them? Well, I believe Jesus has made it simple for us by saying,

"You shall love the Lord your God with all your heart, and with all your soul, and with all your mind. This is the first and great commandment. And the second [is] like unto it, you shall love your neighbor as yourself. <u>On these two commandments hang all the law and the prophets.</u>" (Matthew 22:37-40)

What He is telling us here is that when we allow the love of God to lead us and direct all our thoughts and actions, we will fulfill the other laws automatically. When you love God with all your heart, soul, mind and strength, you will not have any other Gods before Him, you will not worship idols and you will not take His name in vain. When you love your neighbor as yourself, you will not lie to him or about him, you will not steal from him, and you certainly will not kill him.

Paul put it even more strongly. He said

"...for whatsoever [is] not of faith is sin. " (Romans 14:23)

When you first become a Christian, you realize that things like killing, stealing, lying, etc. are wrong. As you come to know the Lord, and begin to love Him more, you become more sensitive to who He is and what grieves Him. Things that you previously had not noticed have now become unacceptable to you, because you know it grieves Him, and to grieve Him grieves you. It breaks your fellowship with Him and causes you to lose the sense of His abiding presence. Once you become accustomed to His presence, you find that the lack of his presence - or seeming lack, He never leaves - makes you very unhappy. When you love someone you want to please them and whatever displeases them displeases you. This is the way we grow and learn. It becomes a matter of pleasing God, not merely following rules. It is a matter of a living, vital relationship with the Creator of the Universe, Who has called us to be holy because He is holy. (Leviticus 11:44)

Jesus said,

"If you love me, keep my commandments." (John 14:15)

And His commandments are not grievous or burdensome. (I John 5:3) They are instructions as to how to live in order to obtain the blessings He desires to bestow on us. His will for us is for us to prosper and be in good health and for our soul to prosper (III John 1:2) and His commandments to us are instructions in how to live so that that can happen.

How do we learn His commandments? By reading the Bible, which is His expressed will toward to us, and by spending time in His presence until we can clearly hear His voice. Jesus has promised us

"My sheep hear my voice, and I know them, and they follow me" (John 10:27)

He has promised that if we trust Him and commit our way to him and keep His commandments that He will direct our path and our lives will be blessed.

My son, forget not my law; but let your heart keep my commandments:
For length of days, and long life, and peace, shall they add to you?
So shall thou find favor and good understanding in the sight of God and man.
Trust in the LORD with all your heart; and lean not unto your own understanding.
In all thy ways acknowledge him, and he shall direct your paths. (Proverbs 3:1,2,4-6)

Sometimes when we have been engaged in a particular sin for a long time it is not easy to stop. Why is this?

The Bible tells us:

Know ye not, that to whom ye yield yourselves servants to obey, his servants ye are to whom ye obey; whether of sin unto death, or of obedience unto righteousness? (Romans 6:16)

This means when we yield to sin we become the servant, or slave, to sin. We begin by having the power to choose whether or not to engage in an action, but if we continue to yield to it, we find that it gains power over us until we no longer have the power to refuse it. This is why certain sins are sometimes called "vices".

Through Christ, we are made free from former bondages so that we can freely serve Him.

But God be thanked, that ye were the servants of sin,
but ye have obeyed from the heart that form of
doctrine which was delivered you.
Being then made free from sin, ye became the servants
of righteousness.
I speak after the manner of men because of the infirmity
of your flesh: for as ye have yielded your members
servants to uncleanness and to iniquity unto
iniquity; even so now yield your members servants
to righteousness unto holiness. (Romans 6:17,19)

This means that as you <u>were</u> the servants of sin, before you knew Christ, and as you yielded your body to sin, now that you are in Christ, you yield your body to righteousness. It is a choice you make daily. Walking in complete deliverance takes time. You didn't become addicted to cigarettes, alcohol or sexual sin overnight, and sometimes you don't become free overnight. There are times people do. There are times God, by divine intervention, sets people free in an instant. But, usually it is a matter of continually choosing to say "No", time after time, calling on Him to enable you, until finally the desire leaves for good.

God has given us powerful tools in the battle against temptation – prayer, the Word, the Baptism in the Holy Spirit, and fasting – all of which are discussed in detail in the following chapters.

Remember, it is one thing to be honestly committed to live for Jesus and fail occasionally (though, hopefully, less and less often), but it is another thing to just give in and give up. Be assured that if you honestly trust Him, and are seriously committed to live for Him, He will not fail you. And He will forgive you when you fail, and encourage you, and lead you on to ultimate victory.

Maybe you think, "I am not really all that bad, I have never done any of those things".

The Bible tells us all have sinned and fallen short of the glory of God, and that none of us is righteous as God counts righteousness.

There is none that understandeth, there is none that seeketh after God.

For all have sinned, and come short of the glory of God;
As it is written, There is none righteous, no, not one:
(Romans 3: 10, 11, 23)

Not only that, but in the light of a perfectly holy and just God, the Bible tells us all our righteousness is as filthy rags to a holy God.

But we are all as an unclean thing, and all our righteousnesses are as filthy rags; and we all do fade as a leaf; and our iniquities, like the wind, have taken us away. (Isaiah 64:6)

This is somewhat difficult to understand with our natural minds.

But the natural man receiveth not the things of the

Spirit of God: for they are foolishness unto him: neither can he know them, because they are spiritually discerned. (I Corinthians 2:14)

It is not until our spirit comes into contact with the reality of God, and He begins to enlighten us to His truth, that we can see ourselves in the light of His Glory and know how flawed we are in comparison to our Creator, and how much we need His indwelling presence in our lives to make us everything He created us to be.

If you desire to hear His voice, to know His will for your life and to allow Him to enable you to live a holy life, pray this prayer:

Father God, I thank you that you always hear me. I thank you for loving me and bringing me into your kingdom and I desire to know your will and hear your voice so that I can do your will in every area of my life. Help me to hear your voice, to be able to distinguish it from other voices and empower me to do your will in all things. I desire my life to be pleasing to you and to bring glory to you and I am making the decision today to trust you in all things and listen closely moment by moment so that you may direct my path. I ask these things in the Name of Jesus. AMEN

What is Baptism?

The Greek word *bap-tid'-zo,* translated as "baptism" in the New Testament, means "to whelm" or to "immerse in fluid".

The practice of baptism stems from a ritual in the old covenant. In the tabernacle in the wilderness, only the priests were allowed to enter the presence of God. But before they did, they had to be "sanctified" by washing in a pool which was just outside the door of the tabernacle.

And Aaron and his sons thou shalt bring unto the door of the tabernacle of the congregation, and shalt wash them with water. (Exodus 25:4)

This ritual bath was called a *"mikveh"* and signified being set apart unto God.

The word "baptism" is only used in the New Testament, and the first reference we find is where John the "Baptist" is baptizing people in the River Jordan saying,

I indeed baptize you with water unto repentance: but he that cometh after me is mightier than I, whose shoes I am not worthy to bear: he shall baptize you with the Holy Ghost, and with fire: (Matthew 3:11)

John was referring to Jesus here, who would later come to "baptize you with the Holy Ghost, and with fire".

He also makes the statement that He is baptizing "with

water unto repentance". So we see that water baptism is an outward acknowledgement of the commitment to "repent" or turn from sin and be sanctified, or set apart to God.

Jesus' disciples also baptized in water for the same reason.

After these things came Jesus and his disciples into the land of Judea; and there he tarried with them, and baptized. (John 3:22)

[Note: this passage makes it appear as if John is saying Jesus Himself baptized, but in a later passage he tells us Jesus did not, only His disciples did. (John 4:2)]

Since this verse begins "After these things…" it is enlightening to read the previous verses to see what "things" are being referred to.

For God so loved the world, that he gave his only begotten Son, that whosoever believeth in him should not perish, but have everlasting life.
For God sent not his Son into the world to condemn the world; but that the world through him might be saved.
He that believeth on him is not condemned: but he that believeth not is condemned already, because he hath not believed in the name of the only begotten Son of God.
And this is the condemnation, that light is come into the world, and men loved darkness rather than light, because their deeds were evil.
For every one that doeth evil hateth the light, neither

cometh to the light, lest his deeds should be reproved.

But he that doeth truth cometh to the light, that his deeds may be made manifest, that they are wrought in God. (John 3:16-21)

So we see from the context of what Jesus was talking about previously that being baptized one of Jesus' disciples is a sign that one is turning one's life over to God through faith in His son Jesus Christ.

Jesus referred to this again after He rose from the dead.

He that believeth and is baptized shall be saved; but he that believeth not shall be damned. (Mark 16:16)

This is a totally uncompromising statement. We are left in no doubt after reading this, that to be saved, or reconciled to God, we must not only believe that Jesus is the Son of God, but we must be baptized.

The meaning of the word "baptize" in this passage is two-fold. First of all it refers to the ritual *mikveh* or bath which was adopted in the new covenant as an outward sign of a believer's intention to follow Christ and put off the old life and "put on Christ" in the miracle of the New Birth. But it also refers to the transformation of the spirit or inward man as we are overwhelmed or immersed with the Spirit of God and become one with Him. The primary event here is the latter. The apostle Paul refers to it in this passage,

Therefore if any man be in Christ, he is a new creature: old things are passed away; behold, all things are

become new. (II Corinthians 5:7)

And again,

...ye have put off the old man with his deeds;
And have put on the new man, which is renewed in
knowledge after the image of him that created him:
(Colossians 3:9, 10)

And most emphatic of all,

For as many of you as have been baptized into Christ
have put on Christ. (Galatians 3:27)

When we are baptized into Christ we "put off the 'old
man'" and we "put on Christ".

Know ye not, that so many of us as were baptized into
Jesus Christ were baptized into his death?
Therefore we are buried with him by baptism into
death: that like as Christ was raised up from the dead
by the glory of the Father, even so we also should walk
in newness of life. (Romans 6:3,4)

We see that baptism symbolizes spiritual death of the
"old man" with its sinful nature and desires, and being
"raised" to a new life in Christ by the power of His
resurrection.

I am crucified with Christ: nevertheless I live; yet not I,
but Christ liveth in me: and the life which I now live in
the flesh I live by the faith of the Son of God, who loved
me, and gave himself for me. (Galatians 2:20)

So baptism is a picture of the New Birth. What happens on the inside of us as we are born again can only be communicated by parables or pictures. The Bible refers to it as a "mystery".

To whom God would make known what is the riches of the glory of this mystery among the Gentiles; which is Christ in you, the hope of glory: (Colossians 1:27)

To reiterate, the *mikveh* or washing of the priests in the Old Covenant signified a ritual "cleansing" or sanctification to make one fit to enter the presence of God. Baptism in the New Covenant is similarly an act of sanctification to prepare one for the presence of God. But where the priest in the old covenant entered into the presence of God in the temple temporarily, the believer in the New Covenant receives the presence of God by the infilling of the Holy Spirit which remains for eternity.

The Hebrew word *mikveh*, like the Greek word *baptidzo* for baptize, means a total immersion. When we are born again we are totally immersed in and transformed by the presence and the of power God.

Therefore if any man be in Christ, he is a new creature: old things are passed away; behold, all things are become new. (II Corinthians 5:17)

Jesus told the disciples,

And I will pray the Father, and he shall give you another Comforter, that he may abide with you forever;

*Even the Spirit of truth; whom the world cannot
receive, because it seeth him not, neither knoweth
him: but ye know him; for he dwelleth with you, and
shall be in you.* (John 14:16, 17)

He was speaking of the Holy Spirit who would be sent
to indwell them after His death and resurrection, who is
one in being with Himself and the Father. Notice He
says "you know him, for he dwelleth (lives) with you,
and shall be in you".

He also said,

*Go ye therefore, and teach all nations, baptizing them
in the name of the Father, and of the Son, and of
the Holy Ghost:*
*Teaching them to observe all things whatsoever I have
commanded you: and, lo, I am with you always,
even unto the end of the world. Amen.* (Matthew
28:19, 20)

We see here that Jesus has promised He will never
leave us. We need to live our lives according to this
truth. We also see that we are to teach all that He has
commanded us. We are to teach people to be separated
to God through His Son Jesus Christ. As Christians and
followers of Christ, we are to share the gospel (good
news) that Jesus has come to heal, save and deliver all
who come to Him and to live our lives in a way which
will be a living example of this truth.

Why should I read the Bible?

As newborn babes, desire the sincere milk of the word, that you may grow thereby (I Peter 2:2)

The Bible tells us that reading the Word nourishes our spirit. When we are newly "born again" we are a baby in the things of the spirit. The Word is our spiritual food. Jesus said:

... "It is written, Man shall not live by bread alone, but by every word that proceeds out of the mouth of God." (Matthew 4:4)

The Word of God is the means by which we acquire knowledge of God and mature in the things of God. How does this work?

In the beginning was the Word, and the Word was with God, and the Word was God. (John 1:1)

The Bible tells us that God's Word and Himself are inseparable. It goes on to say,
And the Word was made flesh, and dwelt among us, (and we beheld his glory, the glory as of the only begotten of the Father,) full of grace and truth. (John 1:14)

This verse is talking about Jesus, the only begotten son of the Father, who is the Word of God made flesh. In other words, the Living Word. When we read the Word of God we are actually partaking of His nature. We are "feeding" our spirit. We are partaking of Jesus, Himself. This is one of the ways we manifest his having made us one with Him. Jesus was speaking of this when He said,

"I am the living bread which came down from heaven: if any man eat of this bread, he shall live forever" (John 6:51)

He further says,

"...the words that I speak unto you, they are spirit, and they are life." (John 6:63)

He is telling us that the Word is life. This is a very strong statement. To be more explicit, the Bible tells us we are "spirit, soul and body".

...and I pray God your whole spirit and soul and body be preserved blameless unto the coming of our Lord Jesus Christ. (I Thessalonians 5:23)

We *are* a spirit, we *have* a soul, and we *inhabit* a body. Our body is what connects us to this world, our spirit is what connects us to God, and our soul connects our spirit to our body. Our soul consists of our mind, our will and our emotions. Until we are "born again" and recreated in the image and likeness of God the Father, our soul has nothing to connect it to God and so it connects to anything which appeals to it. Once we are born again, our recreated spirit connects us to God, and we have to "feed" it on spiritual "food" to strengthen that connection. We do this by prayer and reading God's Word.

The book of Proverbs tells us,

The spirit of a man will sustain his infirmity; but a wounded spirit who can bear? (Proverbs 18:14)

In other words, our spirit will strengthen our physical body, but if our spirit is weak, we have nothing within us with which to strengthen ourselves.

Furthermore, the apostle Paul tells us,

"For the word of God is quick, and powerful, and sharper than any two-edged sword, piercing even to the dividing asunder of soul and spirit, and of the joints and marrow, and is a discerner of the thoughts and intents of the heart." (Hebrews 4:12)

This is a powerful statement. He is telling us that it is the Word of God which enables us to distinguish between our soul and our spirit. Why is this important? Well, it is how we know when the Holy Spirit is talking to us through our spirit, or if the thoughts which we think are coming from Him are only coming from our own mind or even from other spirits. (We will talk about these in another chapter)

He also says that the Word is a "discerner of the thoughts and intents of the heart." In other words the Word helps us to judge our thoughts and intentions according to God's righteous judgment. When we make a habit of reading the Word we can no longer deceive ourselves and rationalize bad thoughts or behavior. The Word raises a standard by which to judge ourselves so that we can be guided by God's standards rather than our own.

We read in the following passage that "taking heed to" or paying attention to the Word of God enables us to lead a holy life.

Wherewithal shall a young man cleanse his way? by taking heed thereto according to thy word. (Psalm 119:9)

And again:

Thy word have I hid in mine heart, that I might not sin against thee. (Psalms 119:11)

We "hide the word in our hearts" by reading it, meditating on it and learning it "by heart". It can then lead us in right paths.

The book of Proverbs tells us that the Word will direct us and guide us.

Thy word is a lamp unto my feet, and a light unto my path. (Proverbs 119:105)

These verses from Proverbs go even farther:

My son, attend to my words; incline thine ear unto my sayings.
Let them not depart from thine eyes; keep them in the midst of thine heart.
For they are life unto those that find them, and health to all their flesh.. (Proverbs 4:20-22)

Here we see that not only is the Word life to our spirit, but it is health to our physical body.

We see this again in Psalms:

He sent his word, and healed them (Psalms 107:20)

So to summarize, we see that we need to read the Word to grow up into a mature Christian and to be able to appropriate all that God would give us through our relationship with Him. Does this sound like a chore? You will find, on the contrary, that as you give yourself over to God and spend time fellowshipping with Him in His Word, it will become your greatest joy and delight. You will continually be discovering ways your Heavenly Father wants to bless your life and in the Word you will find faith to receive these blessings as we are told,

So then faith cometh by hearing, and hearing by the word of God. (Romans 10:17)

And we see that building our faith is yet another blessing by which we can benefit by reading the Word. In order to really understand all that you are in Christ and all that He has done for you by His sacrifice on the cross, it is essential to read the entire Bible. No, not all at once! Just little by little each day.

All Scripture is given by inspiration of God, and is
    profitable for doctrine, for reproof, for correction,
    for instruction in righteousness:
That the man of God may be perfect, thoroughly
    furnished unto all good works.
    (II Timothy 3:16, 17)

The Greek word *ar'-tee-os* translated as "perfect"

means "complete" or "mature". Reading the Word will help to mature us in the knowledge of God and enable us to do the works of God.

We are also told to study the scriptures to show ourselves approved to God, that we might "rightly divide the word of truth", in other words to clearly interpret the Word, that we need not be ashamed.

Study to show thyself approved unto God, a workman that needeth not to be ashamed, rightly dividing the word of truth. (II Timothy 2:15)

As Christians, we should be able to explain our faith to others and answer questions they have about the Bible. We are Christ's ambassadors.

Now then we are ambassadors for Christ...
(II Corinthians 5 ;20)

In other words, we represent Christ to the world, to the people around us who don't know Him. We need to know the Word to do that effectively.

The Bible tells us when the children of Israel were wandering in the wilderness for forty years they ate "manna", or bread, which came down from heaven.

Then said the LORD unto Moses, Behold, I will rain bread from heaven for you; and the people shall go out and gather a certain rate every day, that I may prove them, whether they will walk in my law, or no....
...and in the morning the dew lay round about the host.

And when the dew that lay was gone up, behold,
upon the face of the wilderness there lay a small
round thing, as small as the hoar frost on the
ground.
And the house of Israel called the name thereof Manna:
and it was like coriander seed, white; and the taste
of it was like wafers made with honey.
(Exodus 16:4,13,14)

We see that the manna was small and round like
coriander seed. It was white, and it tasted like wafers
made with honey. Each day they would go out first
thing in the morning and gather just enough for one
day. They could not save it for the next day or it would
rot.

Notwithstanding they hearkened not unto Moses; but
some of them left of it until the morning, and it bred
worms, and stank: and Moses was wroth with them.
(Exodus 16:19)

Now, Jesus tells us He is the bread which came down
from Heaven.

I am the living bread which came down from heaven: if
any man eat of this bread, he shall live forever: and the
bread that I will give is my flesh, which I will give for
the life of the world. (John 6:51)

And we also know that Jesus is the Living Word.
When we read the Word we are eating the "bread of
life". We are partaking of Jesus Himself. And
according to the pattern given to us in the Bible, we
need to do this first thing in the morning each day. We
need to spend time with Jesus, reading the Word and

just fellowshipping with Him, praying and listening to what He says to our hearts, so that we can receive our spiritual food, which is the wisdom we need to carry us through the day. In addition to this, spending this time with Him causes us to become sensitive to him and tune in to him so that we can be aware of Him leading and directing us all through the day.

As you begin to spend time in the Word with Him on a daily basis, your life will take on a meaning and a significance you never thought possible. Small things become charged with joy. Things which never seemed to matter become terrifically important when they become things you share with your Lord as He infuses them with His life.

Commit today to go all the way with Jesus and allow Him to permeate every aspect of your life so that you are no longer bound by your natural limitations, but you release His supernatural power into every area of your life.

If you would like to begin today to allow the Lord to lead and direct your life by the wisdom of His Living Word pray this prayer:

Father God, Loving Savior, Creator of the Universe, I commit today to grow closer to you each day by spending time with you in your presence and in your Word. Please order my time to make this possible. Thank you for your boundless love for me and your ceaseless attention to every detail of my life. I thank you that I can confidently count on your leading and guiding me and your eternal faithfulness, through Christ my Lord. AMEN

What is Faith?

We hear a lot about faith, and most people have an idea of what it means, but you can't really put your faith to work for you until you understand what the Bible means by faith.

Faith is a very important concept. It is so important that the Bible tells us four times,

"The just shall live by faith" (Habakkuk 2:4, Romans 1:17, Galatians 3:11, Hebrews 10:38)

And even more strongly put,

"Whatever is not of faith is sin" (Romans 4:13)

If faith is so important, it would seem that it would profit us to know as much about it as we possibly can.

Both the Hebrew word *em-oo-naw* and the Greek word *pis'-tis* used for faith in these passages can be translated as "truth" and "moral conviction" or "trust". So we see the word faith carries the implication of believing in, or trusting in, the truth. I think we can safely say that it is believing the Word is true. Indeed, Jesus said to the Father *"Thy Word is Truth"* (John 17:17)

But you say, of course I believe the Word is true. Well, we say that, but many times our words and our actions show we don't really believe it.

For example, suppose you have just read in the Word

where Jesus said, *Whatsoever ye shall ask the Father in my name, he will give it* [to] *you.* (John 16:23) and you pray and ask the Father in Jesus name to send you the money to pay the phone bill. A little while later one of your friends asks you how you are and you burst into tears saying they are going to shut off your phone. This isn't faith is it? No, faith is believing that if I read it in the Word, then it is true. Jesus said if I ask, He will do it, so He will do it. Period.

But faith is more than just believing. The Bible tells us,

"As ye have therefore received Christ Jesus the Lord, so walk ye in him" . (Colossians 2:6)

We know that we received Christ by faith, and we know we are to walk in faith, and this is telling us we walk in faith the same way we received Jesus. How did we do that? Well, first we had to believe that He is who He is. The Bible tells us,

"...if thou shalt confess with thy mouth the Lord Jesus, and shalt believe in thine heart that God hath raised him from the dead, thou shalt be saved."
(Romans 10:10)

When we received Christ, it wasn't enough just to believe that He is who He is. The Bible tells us even the devils believe that He is who He is, (James 2:29) but we had to speak it with our mouth. We must continue to "walk in faith" the same way, by not only believing the truth of the word but by speaking it.

There is a good example of faith in operation in the

eleventh chapter of the Gospel of Mark. Jesus and the disciples were walking along and Jesus was hungry and would have eaten figs from a fig tree but the Bible tells us "the time for figs was not yet" so there were no figs on the tree. Then Jesus said to the fig tree, *"No one will ever eat fruit from you again"* (Mark 11:14)

The next day they were walking by the fig tree and the disciples noticed the fig tree was dried up by the roots. When the disciples commented on this Jesus said, *"Have faith in God."* (Mark 11:22)

This is more accurately translated "Have the faith *of* God" or "Have God's kind of faith". The next two verses explain how we do that.

For verily I say unto you, That whosoever shall say unto this mountain, Be thou removed, and be thou cast into the sea; and shall not doubt in his heart, but shall believe that those things which he saith shall come to pass; he shall have whatsoever he saith. (Mark 11:23)

He is saying here that whoever <u>says</u> to the mountain "Be cast into the sea" and does not doubt in his heart, but believes the thing he <u>says</u> will come to past, will have whatever he <u>says</u>. Notice he uses the word "says" here three times, and He only uses the word "believes" one time. I think we can safely assume that what we say is as important as what we believe.

The truth is that what we say proves what we believe.

There is also a spiritual principle being demonstrated here.

Recall, Jesus said "Have faith in God" which we have already said can be interpreted to mean, "Have the God-kind of faith" or have faith like God has.

Notice Jesus' faith. When He cursed the fig tree, he just walked away confidant of what would happen. When he saw it was dead the next day he wasn't surprised. It was what He expected.

God created the universe in exactly the same way. He simply spoke and it was. He said "Light be" and light was. (Genesis 1:3) and He continued to create merely by speaking the words. [Read all of Chapter 1 in the Book of Genesis to see the whole story of creation]

This passage carries this principle even further:

God who at sundry times and in divers manners spake in time past unto the fathers by the prophets,

Hath in these last days spoken unto us by his Son, whom he hath appointed heir of all things, by whom also he made the worlds

Who being the brightness of his glory, and the express image of his person, and upholding all things by the word of his power. (Hebrews 1:1-3)

We see from this that the world was not only created by the Word, but is continually "upheld" or held together, by the Word. But not just by the Word alone, but by its being spoken aloud. And this is where we come in.

We see that God created the universe by speaking His word into it. The Bible then tells us that He created us in His image. What does this mean? Well first of all, God is a spirit and we are spirits. But there is more.

God speaks, and what He speaks is. It is just that simple. And being created in His image, (Genesis 1:26) what we speak is. In other words, we too, like God, have what we say. You think that maybe this is a little radical?

Let's look again at what Jesus said.

For verily [truly] I say unto you, That whosoever shall say unto this mountain, Be thou removed, and be thou cast into the sea; and shall not doubt in his heart, but shall believe that those things which he saith shall come to pass; he shall have whatsoever he saith. (Mark 11:23)

This is Jesus talking here, and He is saying that "whosoever" [Are you a whosoever? I am; and I think you are too.] shall have "whatsoever" [whatsoever means anything you want it to mean] he says. "Whosoever" will have "whatsoever" he says. More simply still, He is saying we have what we say when we believe what we say is true, just like God does.

The difference between God and us is that God always says what is perfect, true, just and pure, and He says the same thing all the time. In other words, He doesn't say one thing one day, and the opposite the next. We, on the other hand, until we learn otherwise, say pretty well what we feel like - good, bad, or indifferent. And usually we are not really very consistent. But when we begin to take control of our tongue and allow the Holy Spirit to direct our thoughts and words according to the Word of God, then what we say is in agreement with what God has already said. Then it is not just our words alone, but also our words in agreement with His Words which have already been spoken, and He is able to empower our Words to come to pass more quickly.

We need to get hold of this and keep it in mind. The devil cannot create anything. All he can do is to pervert, or twist, what God has created into evil purposes. Fear is faith perverted. Faith is believing the truth and speaking it into existence. Fear is believing a lie, or something contrary to God's Word, and speaking it into existence. Notice Jesus said "whosoever" will have "whatsoever" he says. Not "certain good people will have certain good things". You have probably heard of people who have said of their children, "They will never amount to anything". And usually, they never do. Or you have heard people say [hopefully not yourself] "I can never have anything. As soon as I get any extra money, I get an extra bill". And this is what happens.

Proverbs tells us,

Death and life are in the power of the tongue: and they that indulge it shall eat the fruit thereof. (Proverbs 18:21 JPS)

So we see that controlling what we say is as vital to faith as what we believe. Having established that we need to focus on what we believe. Or rather, how we believe.

Recall Mark 11:23. Jesus said,
For verily [truly] *I say unto you, That whosoever shall say unto this mountain, Be thou removed, and be thou*

cast into the sea; and <u>shall not doubt in his heart, but</u>
<u>shall believe that those things which he saith shall come</u>
<u>to pass;</u> he shall have whatsoever he saith.

He says we need to have no doubt, but believe the
things we say will come to pass. How do we acquire
that kind of confidence?

The writer of Hebrews puts it this way:

Now faith is the substance of things hoped for, the
evidence of things not seen. (Hebrews 11:1)

The "substance" of "things hoped for" means of which
the things we are hoping for are made. We are told that
visible things are made of invisible things, or the things
we can see are made of things we cannot see.

Through faith we understand that the worlds were
framed by the word of God, so that things which are
seen were not made of things which do appear.
(Hebrews 11:3)

In other words, the world was created by the Word of
God and the visible things are made of invisible things,
namely words spoken in faith.

But the kind of confidence that is needed to empower
words spoken in faith is more than just mental assent; it
is a supreme confidence in the fact that if God said it, it
is truth.

An example of this kind of faith is given by Abraham
whom God told would be the "father of many nations"

even though he was 100 years old and his wife Sarah was past the age of having children. But the Bible tells us,

He staggered not at the promise of God through unbelief; but was strong in faith, giving glory to God; And being fully persuaded that, what he (God) *had promised, he was able also to perform.* (Romans 4:20,21)

Abraham "staggared not at the promise of God through unbelief". This means he didn't waiver in his belief, but was "strong in faith" being "<u>fully persuaded</u>" that what God had promised He was able to do.
We need to be "fully persuaded" that what God has promised He is able to do.

How can we do that? First of all we need to know what God has promised, and we can find that by reading the Word. Just as God promised Abraham He would make him the father of many nations, there are promises in the Bible, which God has made for us. But we will never know that He has made them until we read the Bible and find them. Also, by reading the Word we find examples of what God has done in the past for ordinary people just like us who have trusted Him and believed His Word. This builds our confidence that what He has done before He will do again. This is why the Bible tells us that *"Faith cometh by hearing, and hearing by the Word of God"* (Romans 10:17)

So, we see that reading the Bible is essential to growing in faith, and growing in faith is essential to receiving the promises of God in our lives. But we also must speak our faith:

But the righteousness which is of faith speaketh on this wise…
But what saith it? The word is nigh thee, even in thy mouth, and in thy heart: that is, the word of faith, which we preach; (Romans 10:6,8)

So faith "speaks". And what does it speak? It speaks the Word. The Greek word *kay-roos'-so* translated as "preach" means to "proclaim divine truth". So when we speak the Word in faith we are proclaiming it as truth. When we proclaim God's Word as truth, the circumstances will have to align themselves with the truth. Every knee must bow at the Name of Jesus when we come in His Name with His authority proclaiming His truth. (Philippians 2:10)

We read in the Gospel of Mark that when the apostles first began to proclaim the truth of the Gospel after Jesus had ascended into Heaven, the Lord confirmed the Word with miracles.

And they went forth, and preached every where, the Lord working with them, and confirming the word with signs following. (Mark 16:20)

The "signs" follow the preaching (or proclaiming) of the Word. When we proclaim the Word, God will confirm it with "signs following" also. God is not a respecter of persons. (Acts 10:34) What He did for them, He will do for us. But we cannot expect to see signs following reciting our symptoms, or rehearsing our problems. No, signs follow proclaiming the Word alone. So let's make sure that our words are His Words and that what we speak is truth.

This does not mean denying circumstances. It means taking no account of them. The Bible tells us concerning Abraham:

And being not weak in faith, he considered not his own body now dead, when he was about a hundred years old, neither yet the deadness of Sarah's womb: (Romans 4:19)

Abraham didn't deny his or Sarah's ages, he just didn't consider them.

The Word goes on to say,
He staggered not at the promise of God through unbelief; but was strong in faith, giving glory to God;
And being fully persuaded that, what he (God) *had promised, he was able also to perform.* (Romans 4:20, 21)

We see he was "fully persuaded" that what God had promised, He was able to perform. And so must we be. Notice that it says he was "strong in faith, giving glory to God". When we are strong in faith, we too give glory to God.

Father God, today, I commit today to become a person of faith. I desire to devote myself to reading your Word so that I will know your perfect will for my life and I commit myself to take control of my words speaking only those things which glorify you and allow you to bless my life according to your will. I ask you to order my time to spend time with you in your Word, and open my understanding that I may see your will for my life in your Word. Thank you for showing me the way to be all that you desire me to be and to receive all that you have in store for me that my life can be an example to others of the Loving Heavenly Father that you are, in Jesus' Name. AMEN

Why do I need to pray?

The first reason we need to pray is that the Bible tells us to.

Jesus told the disciples in the garden,

"Watch and pray, that ye enter not into temptation: the spirit indeed is willing, but the flesh is weak".
 (Matthew 26:41)

So, we need to pray to not enter into temptation. He also mentions this when the disciples asked Him to teach them how to pray and He answered them by praying what we refer to as "The Lord's Prayer".

"Our Father which art in heaven, Hallowed be thy name.
Thy kingdom come.
Thy will be done in earth, as it is in heaven.
Give us this day our daily bread.
And forgive us our debts, as we forgive our debtors.
And lead us not into temptation, but deliver us from evil: For thine is the kingdom, and the power, and the glory forever AMEN" (Matthew 6:9,13)

There was a time, not too long ago, when this prayer was prayed each morning in every school in this country. At that time teachers were asked what were the most difficult discipline problems in the schools. The most prevalent answers were talking in class, litter, inappropriate hair (by the way, these hairstyles would be considered very conservative today) and chewing gum. A far cry from assault, rape and shootings. Do you think there is any connection ? (!)

Let's examine this prayer. Jesus is outlining a pattern that we should follow. First, we need to acknowledge our Heavenly Father and His Holiness. Then we pray for His kingdom to come and His will to be done, "on earth as it is in Heaven." This is a powerful principle that many Christians have missed over the centuries. God's will for us is for it to be on earth as it is in Heaven. If you can only get hold of this concept, you will have grasped something that many Christians seem to have failed to see. If Heaven is to be the standard by which we gage our prayers, then can we confidently pray for healing of all sickness? Well is there sickness in Heaven? I don't think so. Then it would seem that God wants us well and we can confidently pray for Him to heal us from any sickness or disease. Is there any poverty or lack in Heaven? I don't think so. The Bible tells us the streets are made of gold. (Revelation 21:21) So, it follows that we can pray for God to provide all our needs. As a matter of fact, the Bible tells us

"But my God shall supply all your need according to his riches in glory by Christ Jesus". (Philippians 4:19)

So, God will provide all our needs. It also tells us,

Bless the LORD, O my soul, and forget not all his benefits:
Who forgiveth all thine iniquities; who healeth all thy diseases; (Psalm 103:3)

So, God will heal all our diseases.

But we have to ask. James tells us,

"You have not because you ask not." (James 4:2)

Jesus goes on to pray "Forgive us our debts as we forgive our debtors". Other translations read, "Forgive us our trespasses as we forgive those who trespass against us". This simply means we need to pray each day for God to forgive us when we fail Him and fall short of the way we know we should live, but we must be careful to forgive those who have hurt us also. Notice He says "as we forgive those..." God forgives us according to how we forgive others.

Jesus mentions this in another place.

And when ye stand praying, forgive, if ye have aught against any: that your Father also which is in heaven may forgive you your trespasses.
But if ye do not forgive, neither will your Father which is in heaven forgive your trespasses. (Mark 11:25,26)

Forgiveness is an essential condition of answered prayer. We have to constantly guard our hearts against bitterness, resentment and unforgiveness to allow unhindered fellowship with the Father.

And then we come again to *"And lead us not into temptation, but deliver us from evil"*. Leading a holy life isn't easy, but it is simple. We just have to ask the Father to lead us in the way He would have us to go. Not only is it not easy, it is impossible without Him.

But, we can be sure that if we trust Him and ask Him, He will enable us to do the impossible with His help. God has commanded us:

Sanctify yourselves therefore, and be ye holy: for I am the LORD your God. (Leviticus 20:7)

And God is never unreasonable. He will never command us to do anything that He will not enable us to do.

... The things which are impossible with men are possible with God. (Luke 18:27)

The apostle Paul asks us to pray for all men, in particular those that are in authority, that we may be able to live peaceful, godly lives:

I exhort therefore, that, first of all, supplications, prayers, intercessions, and giving of thanks, be made for all men;
For kings, and for all that are in authority; that we may lead a quiet and peaceable life in all godliness and honesty. (I Timothy 2:1,2)

James tells us,

Is any among you afflicted? let him pray. (James 5:13)

The Greek word *kak-op-ath-eh'-o* means to have hardships or trouble. So we are to pray when we have hardships, or trouble. But how should we pray? Should we pray just for strength to bear them with cheerfulness and put up a good front? Or should we pray to get free of them?

Well, we can find the answer to that in the Bible also.

Many are the afflictions of the righteous: but the LORD delivereth him out of them all. (Psalms 34:19)

It says He will deliver us out of them all. That is pretty clear isn't it? But, you say, it is the "righteous" that the Lord will deliver, and you are not sure that means you? Let's look at what the apostle Paul says about that.

For he hath made him to be sin for us, who knew no sin; that we might be made the righteousness of God in him. (II Corinthians 5:21)

He is saying that we are the righteousness of God in Christ, who became sin for us. In other words, He became sin on our behalf. He took our sin to give us His righteousness. This means we qualify to have God deliver us from ALL our afflictions. (Look back again at Psalms 34:19)

Then James goes on to say

Elijah was a man subject to like passions as we are, and he prayed earnestly that it might not rain: and it rained not on the earth by the space of three years and six months.
And he prayed again, and the heaven gave rain, and the earth brought forth her fruit. (James 5:18,19)

I like this scripture. He says Elijah was a man subject to the same weakness as we are, and yet when he prayed he stopped the rain for three years and six months, and when he prayed, again it rained. I love these stories in the Bible that show how God used people just like us, because if He used them, He can use us. I don't know about you, but I want to be a person God can use to pray for whatever He wants done on this earth in my lifetime.

The apostle Paul tells us *"Pray without ceasing."* (I Thessalonians 5:17) This is pretty strong; we are to pray all the time. How do we do that? Well this idea pretty much embodies what being a Christian is all about. When we allow ourselves to become so conscious of the presence of God on the inside of us that we continually let Him be the arbiter of everything we do, always listening for His voice or watching to see if we feel a check in our spirit where the Holy Spirit is telling us to change direction, then we will be doing what the Bible refers to as "walking in the Spirit". This is a life filled with such joy and such peace that the details of our lives no longer have to power to disturb us. When we get a bill in the mail, we don't have to panic wondering how we can pay it. We have the confidence that God has already made a way, we only have to ask. When we get a pain or some sort of physical symptom, we don't have to wonder what disease we are trying to come down with, we only have to pray and whatever it is God will heal us.

David (who wrote the Psalms) talked about that here:

The righteous shall be in everlasting remembrance.
He shall not be afraid of evil tidings: his heart is fixed,
trusting in the LORD. (Psalm 112:7)

We need to "fix" our heart to trust in the Lord. The Hebrew word *koon* translated as "fixed" means to be "established, or firm". If our hearts are "fixed" on the Word, trusting in the Lord, we will not be afraid of bad news, we will be confident that what the Lord has promised, He will perform.

I hope by now you are beginning to get the picture that prayer is more than just reciting something you learned as a child, or calling out to God in a panic-stricken emergency. It is a lifestyle. It is constant communion with your Heavenly Father. It is exercising your privilege as a Child of God spending time with the one who created you and has your best interest at heart as no one else can do, growing in the knowledge and appreciation of Who He is and all that He has for you, both in this life and the one to come. It is feasting at His table and sitting at His feet being taught by His Spirit and being lost in His Love.

Thou wilt show me the path of life: in thy presence is fullness of joy; at thy right hand there are pleasures forevermore. (Psalms 16:11)

It just doesn't get any better than this!

Father God, I come to you. Teach me to hear your voice, to walk in your ways, to grow closer to you each day, and to know your will in every situation. Let me be the instrument you can use to pray out your plan for my life and for the lives of the people around me. Use me to show them your love and care and to draw them to you. Be glorified in my life today and every day. Through Christ my Lord AMEN.

Why do we pray in Jesus' Name?

Jesus Himself told us,

*And whatsoever ye shall ask <u>in my name</u>, that will I do,
    that the Father may be glorified in the Son.
If ye shall ask any thing <u>in my name</u>, I will do it.*
(John 14:13,14)

*Ye have not chosen me, but I have chosen you, and
    ordained you, that ye should go and bring forth
    fruit, and that your fruit should remain: that
    whatsoever ye shall ask of the Father <u>in my name</u>,
    he may give it you.* (John 15:16)

*And in that day ye shall ask me nothing. Verily, verily, I
    say unto you, Whatsoever ye shall ask the Father <u>in
    my name</u>, he will give it you.
Hitherto have ye asked nothing <u>in my name</u>: ask, and ye
    shall receive, that your joy may be full.*
(John 16:23,24)

Here we have Jesus' own Word for it, whatever we ask
the Father in His Name He will do.

But why is that? What is so special about praying in
Jesus' Name?

The Bible tells us that Jesus has been given the Name
that is above all names.

Wherefore God also hath highly exalted him [Jesus],
and given him a name which is above every name:
(Philippians 2:9)

Now Jesus said to his disciples,

All power is given unto me in heaven and in earth. Go ye therefore... (Matthew 28:18)

The Greek word *ex-oo-see'-ah* translated here as "power" literally means "authority". So He is saying that all authority in Heaven and earth has been given to Him, therefore **we** are to go... Go and do what? We see this same event recorded in the Gospel of Mark this way. Jesus said,

Go ye into all the world, and preach the gospel to every creature.
He that believeth and is baptized shall be saved; but he that believeth not shall be damned.
And these signs shall follow them that believe; <u>In my name</u> shall they cast out devils; they shall speak with new tongues;
They shall take up serpents; and if they drink any deadly thing, it shall not hurt them; they shall lay hands on the sick, and they shall recover.
(Mark 16:16-18)

There it is again "in My Name". And what are we to do? Go into all the world and preach the gospel to every creature. And the signs shall follow those that believe in the Name of Jesus are that they will have supernatural power over evil spirits, they shall have supernatural languages, supernatural protection, and supernatural power to heal the sick. These are all things that Jesus did, and now He is commanding believers to do likewise.

What is being described here is a transfer of authority. It is the same type of transfer of authority that takes place when a person is given "power of attorney". When a person is designated as "attorney in fact" for another person this means they have "power of attorney" or legal right to perform legal transactions in the other person's name. Essentially what is happening here is that Jesus is giving those who believe on His name the power of attorney, or the legal right to use His name on this earth. This is the reason the part of the Bible written after His death is referred to as the New "Testament". A testament declares the will of the testator, or the one who writes it, which is to come into effect after the testator dies. Jesus was given "all power in Heaven and earth" but when He left the earth he delegated that authority to us, the believers. But, in order to exercise it we must use His Name, because He is the one to whom it was actually given. We only have the authority to use His Name. But, at that Name, every knee in Heaven and earth and under the earth has to bow.

The Bible goes on to tell us:

Wherefore God also hath highly exalted him [Jesus], and given him a name which is above every name: That at the name of Jesus every knee should bow, of things in heaven, and things in earth, and things under the earth. (Philippians 2:10)

Sickness has a name. But, the Name of Jesus is higher. Poverty has a name. But, the Name of Jesus is higher. Failure has a name. Fear has a name. But, Praise God! the name of Jesus is higher. All these things have to bow at the Name of Jesus.

We have authority to use His name by virtue of the new birth. When we receive Christ by faith and are born again into the Kingdom of God, we are now *in* Christ, and therefore have the legal right to use His Name.

In the book of Acts, we read about a man who had been lame from birth. He was waiting outside the gate (which was called "Beautiful") of the temple. When he saw Peter and Paul he was about to ask them for alms (money) and Peter said to him,

> *Silver and gold have I none; but such as I have give I thee: <u>In the name of Jesus Christ</u> of Nazareth rise up and walk. And he took him by the right hand, and lifted him up: and immediately his feet and ankle bones received strength.*
> *And he leaping up stood, and walked, and entered with them into the temple, walking, and leaping, and praising God.* (Acts 3:6-8)

When Peter commanded him to walk "in the Name of Jesus", immediately he received strength to walk. Then the Bible tells us that the man went into the temple. And all the people in the temple who were used to seeing the lame man every day before the temple came outside to Peter and Paul "greatly wondering". Peter asked them "Why do you marvel at this?" and he began to tell them that Jesus, whom they had delivered up to Pontius Pilate and desired to be crucified, God had raised from the dead. He went on to say,

> *And <u>his name</u> through <u>faith in his name</u> hath made this man strong, whom ye see and know...* (Acts 3:16)

It was faith "in the Name of Jesus" which made the man strong.

The following day the rulers and elders and the high priest had Peter and Paul brought before them and asked them,

By what power, or by what name, have ye done this? (Acts 4:7)

Notice the rulers asked "by what name" did you do this? And Peter and Paul answered,

Be it known unto you all, and to all the people of Israel, that by the name of Jesus Christ of Nazareth, whom ye crucified, whom God raised from the dead, even by him doth this man stand here before you whole. (Acts 4:10)

Again, they took no credit to themselves, but proclaim that it was "by the Name of Jesus Christ" that the man was made whole.

Notice the result of this,

But that it spread no further among the people, let us straitly threaten them, that they speak henceforth to no man in this name. (Acts 4:17)

The rulers forbid them to speak "in this name", the Name of Jesus. They did not forbid Peter and Paul to speak at all, only in the name of Jesus.

So we see that the authority is in the Name of Jesus, not in Peter or Paul for who they were, but in the Name of

Jesus, <u>whose</u> they were. Which is why, since we have been born again and He lives in us (John 14:23), and He has made us one with Himself and the Father (John 17:23), we also have that same authority in His Name. Therefore, as the apostle Paul admonishes us,

And whatsoever ye do in word or deed, <u>do all in the name of the Lord Jesus</u>, giving thanks to God and the Father by him. (Colossians 3:17)

What is the Baptism in the Holy Spirit?

John the Baptist was in Jerusalem baptizing and preaching, saying, "Repent for the Kingdom of Heaven is at hand". And, he said,

I indeed baptize you with water unto repentance: but he that cometh after me is mightier than I, whose shoes I am not worthy to bear: he shall baptize you with the Holy Ghost, and with fire. (Matthew 3:11)

He was speaking of Jesus saying that Jesus would baptize with the Holy Ghost and with fire. After Jesus rose from the dead, He told the disciples,

"Tarry ye in the city of Jerusalem, until ye be endued with power from on high." (Luke 24:49)

They were to wait in Jerusalem until they received "power from on high".

Later we read:

And when the day of Pentecost was fully come, they were all with one accord in one place.
And suddenly there came a sound from heaven as of a rushing mighty wind, and it filled all the
And there appeared unto them cloven tongues like as of <u>fire,</u> and it sat upon each of them.
And they were <u>all filled with the Holy Ghost</u>, and began to speak with other tongues, as the Spirit gave them utterance. (Acts 2:1,4)

Here we see the event that John the Baptist was speaking of when He said that Jesus would "baptize with the Holy Ghost and with fire". The Scripture tells us here that there appeared what looked like "tongues of fire" on each one of them and they were "all filled with the Holy Ghost". Notice the result that they all "began to speak with other tongues, as the Spirit gave them utterance" or as the Holy Spirit gave them the words to speak.

God has not changed. Everything He did in those days, He is still doing now. But we have to receive by faith. Notice the appearance of "tongues of fire" sat on each of them, they were all filled with the Holy Ghost and the wording indicates that they all began to speak with other tongues.

This is not surprising. Let's look again at Jesus final words to the disciples:

And these signs shall follow them that believe; In my name shall they cast out devils; they shall speak with new tongues. (Mark 16:17)

He says these signs shall follow "them that believe". Not just a few chosen special people, but "them that believe". Do you believe? If you do, then this means you.

Here is another reference to this phenomenon. Peter was preaching to some people gathered at the house of Cornelius, a Roman centurion, and as He was speaking the Bible tells us "the Holy Ghost fell on all them that heard the Word". It goes on to say that the Jews were astonished that the Holy Ghost had been poured out on the Gentiles [A Gentile was anyone who was not a Jew. Up until this time all the believers had been Jews]. How did they know the Holy Ghost had been poured out on the Gentiles? It says very clearly:

For they heard them speak with tongues, and magnify God (Acts 10:46)

So, we see that "speaking with tongues", or speaking in a language which one hasn't learned (often referred to as a "prayer language" or "heavenly language") is a sign that one has received the Holy Spirit.

We don't hear a lot about this publicly today, and perhaps this is the first time you have heard of it. But, we can clearly see that this is something that God desires for us.

I want to mention here that many times people think that because they may not have heard of miraculous things taking place that the supernatural things that happened in the early church were only for then and that God just isn't doing these things any more. This could not be farther from the truth. It is beyond the scope of this book to recount the miracles that are taking place in our world today, which you don't hear about in the secular media, but be assured God hasn't changed.

God tells us through the prophet Malachi,

For I the LORD change not (Malachi 3:6)

Also, the writer to the Hebrews writes,
Jesus Christ the same yesterday, and today, and forever. (Hebrews 13:8)

Jesus hasn't changed. What He did two thousand years ago He still does.

Jesus told all the disciples to tarry (wait) in Jerusalem until they would receive power from on high. Was this the first time they had received the Holy Spirit?

No, it wasn't. We see that after Jesus rose from the dead and he appeared to the disciples, the Bible tells us He breathed on them and said, *"Receive the Holy Ghost".* (John 20:22) So they had already received the Holy Ghost, yet Jesus told them to wait in Jerusalem until they would receive "power from on high".

Why was that? Well, when we are born again, the Holy Spirit takes up residence on the inside of us to live within us and transform us into the likeness of Christ, if we will yield to His leading and allow Him to do this.

But the Baptism in the Holy Spirit is an empowering for ministry. The word "baptism" comes from the same Greek word we saw earlier, *bap-tid'-zo*, which means to immerse, or to make fully wet. I have heard one Bible teacher describe it this way. When we are born again, we receive the spirit "within" us, and when we are baptized in the Holy Spirit, we receive the spirit "upon" us. The spirit "within" separates us from the world into Christ. But the spirit "upon" us empowers us to serve Him.

Let's examine this account of the apostle Paul:

Paul having passed through the upper coasts came to Ephesus:

and finding certain disciples,

He said unto them, Have ye received the Holy Ghost since ye believed? And they said unto him, We have not so much as heard whether there be any Holy Ghost.

And he said unto them, Unto what then were ye baptized? And they said, Unto John's baptism.

Then said Paul, John verily baptized with the baptism of repentance, saying unto the people, that they should believe on him which should come after him, that is, on Christ Jesus.

When they heard this, they were baptized in the name of the Lord Jesus.

And when Paul had laid his hands upon them, the Holy Ghost came on them; and they spake with tongues, and prophesied. (Acts 19:1,6)

Notice here that when Paul asked them if they had received the Holy Ghost they told him they had never heard of the Holy Ghost. They hadn't even heard of Jesus but had been baptized into John's baptism. When Paul explained Jesus to them, they were baptized in the Name of Jesus and then <u>afterwards</u> Paul laid his hands on them and it tells us the "Holy Ghost came on them" and they spoke with tongues and prophesied.

When we are "baptized in the Holy Spirit", we are empowered to operate in what the Bible refers to as the "gifts" of the spirit. These gifts are listed as follows:

For to one is given by the Spirit the word of wisdom; to

another the word of knowledge by the same Spirit;

To another faith by the same Spirit; to another the gifts
of healing by the same Spirit;

To another the working of miracles; to another
prophecy; to another discerning of spirits; to
another divers kinds of tongues; to another the
interpretation of tongues.

(I Corinthians 12:8-10)

I will briefly describe these gifts. They are divided loosely into three categories, which are sometimes referred to as the vocal gifts, the power gifts and the gifts of revelation.

The vocal gifts are "divers [different] kinds of tongues [languages]", "interpretation of tongues", and "prophecy".

I want to distinguish here between what is being referred to here as "Divers kinds of tongues" and the prayer language or "unknown" tongue, which you receive when you first receive the baptism in the Holy Spirit. The prayer language you first receive is always accessible. Once you have received it, you can pray in it at any time, as you will. The Holy Spirit will give you the words to pray in your "unknown tongue" any time you chose to yield to Him. It is up to you.

This is such a powerful and important gift I will discuss it in depth in the following chapter. As we have mentioned it is a person speaking in a language they haven't learned as the Holy Spirit gives them utterance" (Acts 2:4) or, rather as the Holy Spirit gives them the words to say. A person operating in this manifestation is praying out God's plan for his own or others' lives, as directed by the Holy Spirit.

The gift of "divers tongues" or "different languages" spoken of here refers to a person given an "utterance" in an unknown tongue in the church which is God speaking through the individual to the church. It is the Holy Spirit speaking *through* one believer to another or others.

"Interpretation of tongues" is not literal translation, or knowing word-for-word what is said, as one does when translating a known language, but it is rather a supernatural impartation of the knowledge of the sense of what is being said by the person speaking in tongues to the listener, to whom the language spoken is also unknown.

"Prophecy" means, literally, to "tell forth" or predict. It is a supernatural speaking forth of events that are to happen. It can also be a clarification of events that are happening and a revelation of God's will pertaining to certain situations. This is usually God speaking to the church, as opposed to the "word of wisdom" which is often to an individual.

The "revelation gifts" are the "word of knowledge", "word of wisdom" and the "discerning of spirits".

The "word of knowledge" is when a person is given revelation of an event that has occurred in the past, frequently regarding another individual, which facilitates ministry to that individual.

The "word of wisdom" is revelation of an event that is going to occur in the future, or guidance or direction pertaining to a course of action that will affect future events, usually for an individual.

"Discerning of spirits" is just what it sounds like. It is the ability to discern what spirits are affecting a given situation in order that we can take authority over them in prayer.

The "power" gifts are the gifts of "healing", "miracles" and "faith".

The gift of "healing" is just what it says. It is supernatural healing of sickness and disease, usually gradual, but sometimes sudden.

The gift of "miracles" is a spontaneous supernatural intervention in natural events. It may also be a miraculously manifested healing. We are beginning to hear of many "creative" miracles recently where God is replacing lost limbs and organs.

The gift of "faith" is miraculous faith, or a superabundant faith. It is supercharged faith that brings ones ability to believe to a dramatically higher level.

These are VERY brief introductory descriptions of these gifts. An intense study of these gifts is beyond the scope of this book, but there are many books and materials available to study them in greater depth.

I particularly want to point out here that while the nine gifts of the Spirit as listed above are manifested as the

Spirit wills (I Corinthians 12:11), the ability to "pray in tongues" is available to anyone who receives the Baptism of the Holy Spirit to utilize at his own will, whenever one chooses. The only choice you have regarding the nine gifts listed above is whether or not to yield to the Holy Spirit and allow Him to manifest them through you. You can refuse to yield to Him, but you cannot force Him to move.

The other vital benefit for a new believer receiving the Baptism of the Holy Spirit is that the Scriptures come alive as the Holy Spirit enables your understanding to comprehend them. This is only logical, as the Bible tells us that the Scriptures were written by men who were "moved by the Holy Spirit" (II Peter 1:21). In other words, it was the Holy Spirit who wrote the Scripture, what better teacher to help you to understand them.

As a matter of fact, the Bible tells us exactly that.

But the anointing which ye have received of him abideth in you, and ye need not that any man teach you: but as the same anointing teacheth you of all things, and is truth, and is no lie, and even as it hath taught you, ye shall abide in him. (I John 2:27)

What John is saying here is that the "anointing" which you have received [the Holy Spirit] lives in you, and you do not need any man to teach you, but the Holy Spirit will teach you all things.

Jesus said the same thing.

*Howbeit when he, the Spirit of truth, is come, he will
guide you into all truth: for he shall not speak of
himself; but whatsoever he shall hear, that shall he
speak: and he will show you things to come.*
(John 16:13)

Jesus is saying here that the "Spirit of truth", or the
Holy Spirit, will guide you into all truth.

This is such an awesome revelation here. You often
hear people use the term the "secret of life", usually in
jest, because most people don't really believe there is
any such thing. But what we are talking about here is
truly the "secret of life".

The secret of the LORD is with them that fear him.
(Psalm 25:14)

We can have an intimate relationship with the Creator
of the Universe and He wants to guide us into "all
truth". I can't imagine anything more worth having
than that.

You are probably wondering, "OK, so I pray and
believe to receive this 'baptism in the Holy Spirit' and I
pray and something I can't understand comes out. How
do I know that is the Holy Spirit giving me the words?"

Jesus answered that question for us too. He said,

*If a son shall ask bread of any of you that is a father,
will he give him a stone? or if he ask a fish, will he
for a fish give him a serpent?
Or if he shall ask an egg, will he offer him a scorpion?*

*If ye then, being evil, know how to give good gifts unto
your children: how much more shall your heavenly
Father give the Holy Spirit to them that ask him?*
(Luke 11:11-13)

I believe He was answering this question here. He is
saying if we ask for bread [bread is symbolic for the
word of God] our Heavenly Father will not give us a
stone. The words we speak, believing the Holy Spirit
(who is God) to be speaking through us, will in fact be
His Words, and not anything else. He goes on to say
that if we ask for fish, he will not give us a serpent, and
if we ask for an egg, he will not give us a scorpion.
Then he says, "How much more will he give the Holy
Spirit to them that ask him?" I think we can take His
Word for it that when we ask for the Holy Spirit, we
can be sure that is what we will get.

Why Tongues?

And when the day of Pentecost was fully come, they
were all with one accord in one place.
And suddenly there came a sound from heaven as of a
rushing mighty wind, and it filled all the house
where they were sitting.
And there appeared unto them cloven tongues like as of
fire, and it sat upon each of them.
And they were all filled with the Holy Ghost, and began
to speak with other tongues, as the Spirit gave them
utterance. (Acts 2:1-4)

We see that when the Holy Spirit first fell and filled
believers He manifested Himself by causing them to
speak in other "tongues" or languages. Why did God
do it this way? Many of us have asked that question
over the years.

I believe the answer can be found in the Epistle of
James. He tells us,

If any man among you seem to be religious, and
bridleth not his tongue, but deceiveth his own
heart, this man's religion is vain. (James 1:26)

The Greek word *khal-in-ag-ogue-eh'-o* translated as
"bridleth" means to "curb" or to "control" ones tongue.
He is saying that if we don't control what we say we
deceive our own heart and our religion is vain, or
useless.

This conveys a powerful concept. The implication is

that what we say influences our "heart" or our attitudes. We usually think of it being the other way around. But Jesus also referred to this relationship of words to attitudes.

Therefore take no thought, saying, What shall we eat? or, What shall we drink? or, Wherewithal shall we be clothed? (Matthew 6:31)

The context here is that he is cautioning against worrying. But notice he equates "taking thought" with "saying". In other words, a thought may come to our mind, but until we put it into words, we do not actually take ownership of it. So, he is saying that what we say is very important.

James goes on to say regarding the tongue,

For in many things we offend all. If any man offend not in word, the same is a perfect man, and able also to bridle the whole body.

Behold, we put bits in the horses' mouths, that they may obey us; and we turn about their whole body.

Behold also the ships, which though they be so great, and are driven of fierce winds, yet are they turned about with a very small helm, whithersoever the governor listeth.

Even so the tongue is a little member, and boasteth great things. Behold, how great a matter a little fire kindleth!

And the tongue is a fire, a world of iniquity; so is the tongue among our members, that it defileth the whole body, and setteth on fire the course of nature; and it is set on fire of hell.

For every kind of beasts, and of birds, and of serpents, and of things in the sea, is tamed, and hath been tamed of mankind:

But the tongue can no man tame; it is an unruly evil, full of deadly poison. (James 3:2-8)

We would do well to just meditate on these verses for a while until we grasp the power that our words have to impact our lives.

Let's just recapitulate here. First of all he says a person who doesn't offend anyone with their words is a "perfect" man and able to control the whole body. The Greek word *tel'-i-os* translated "perfect", could more accurately be translated "mature in integrity or character". I think the implication is obvious. A person who cannot control what they say cannot control their actions. As a man's tongue goes, so his whole body goes.

But the really bad news is this. "But the tongue <u>can no man tame.</u>" He is saying no man can control what they say. Well, what do we do? We submit our tongue to the Holy Spirit and let Him direct what we say. And that is why receiving our prayer language is so important. When we pray in an unknown tongue [our prayer language] the Holy Spirit "gives utterance" or gives us the words to say so that we are praying His words and not our own.

James uses the example of a ship's rudder. The smallest of parts, but as the rudder goes the whole ship goes. And he says similarly the tongue controls the way our body, and ultimately our life, goes. It logically follows that until we have submitted our tongue to the Holy Spirit, we have not totally submitted ourselves to Him.

King Solomon put it this way,

Death and life are in the power of the tongue...
(Proverbs 18:21)

This is a very powerful statement. Jesus made another powerful admonition,

> *But I say unto you, That every idle word that men shall speak, they shall give account thereof in the day of judgment.*
> *For by thy words thou shalt be justified, and by thy words thou shalt be condemned.* (Matthew 12:36,37)

He says we will have to give account of every idle word. That by our words we will be justified or condemned. Why is that? Words are containers. The words we speak contain either blessing or cursing. Recall we found earlier that what we say is what we get. What we are living in today is the result of what we said yesterday. We have been given control of our own destiny and the way we exercise that control is by what we say.

If what we say has such power to affect our lives it is in our best interest to learn to control what we say. But if as James says we cannot control what we say, then what can we do? We can submit our tongues to the Holy Spirit by receiving the baptism of the Holy Spirit

and allow Him to "tame" our tongue.
We are exhorted in the epistle of Jude,

But ye, beloved, building up yourselves on your most holy faith, praying in the Holy Ghost Keep yourselves in the love of God, (Jude 1:20,21)

We see that praying in the Holy Ghost (or Holy Spirit) not only builds our faith, but also keeps us in the love of God.

The apostle Paul makes it plain in this passage that praying "in the spirit" is praying in tongues.

For if I pray in an unknown tongue, my spirit prayeth, but my understanding is unfruitful.
What is it then? I will pray with the spirit, and I will pray with the understanding also.
(I Corinthians 14:14,15)]

He further explains,

He that speaketh in an unknown tongue edifieth himself.
(I Corinthians 14:4)

The Greek word *oy-kod-om-eh'-o* translated here as "edifieth" or "edifies" can be translated as "to erect an edifice or dwelling"

When we consider this passage:

Know ye not that ye are the temple of God, and that the Spirit of God dwelleth in you?
(1 Corinthians 3:16)

As you pray in your prayer language you are making yourself a dwelling place for the Holy Spirit to live on the inside of you. In effect, the more you pray in your prayer language, the more power is imparted to your prayers.

Let's look at this again.

He that speaketh in an unknown tongue edifieth himself. (I Corinthians 14:4)

The Greek word *oy-kod-om-eh'-o* translated here as "edifieth" can also be translated as "instructs".

I really got excited when I saw this the first time. What this means is that when we pray in an "unknown" tongue, the Holy Spirit, who is giving us the words to say, is also "instructing" us. This is not surprising when Jesus has told us,

Howbeit when he, the Spirit of truth, is come, he will guide you into all truth. (John 16:13)

All truth!

And John has said,

But the anointing which ye have received of him abideth in you, and ye need not that any man teach you: but as the same anointing teacheth you of all things, and is truth, and is no lie, and even as it hath taught you, ye shall abide in him. (I John 2:27)

What both of these passages are telling us is that the

Holy Spirit is sent to "instruct" us. Praying in our prayer languages is one of the means He has given us to avail ourselves of this instruction. As you spend time praying in your prayer language, for some time it may seem like nothing is really happening. You may get bored and distracted and wonder if God is really involved in the whole thing. But if you persevere, eventually you will feel flooded with revelation that would take hours to tell or write. Suddenly things you have been concerned about become totally clear and you have the complete confidence that God is taking care of it all. There will usually come to mind a scripture passage that confirms what you are receiving. If you have been praying for guidance concerning a decision you are to make the direction becomes clear. And above all, you are filled with the peace of Christ which "surpasses all understanding".
(Philippians 4:7)

Another reason the apostle Paul gives us for praying in the Spirit is,

Likewise the Spirit also helpeth our infirmities: for we know not what we should pray for as we ought: but the Spirit itself maketh intercession for us with groanings which cannot be uttered. (Romans 8:26)

We see that we don't always know how to pray, or what to pray for, but the Holy Spirit makes intercession for us with "groanings which cannot be uttered". The Greek word *al-al'-ay-tos* translated here as "cannot be uttered," means "unspeakable" or "inexpressible". In other words, they are things that our natural speech is too limited to express, so they can only be expressed in a heavenly language. This is one of the reasons we need to have it.

He goes on to say,

And he that searcheth the hearts knoweth what is the mind of the Spirit, because he maketh intercession for the saints according to the will of God. (Romans 8:27)

Again, He is saying that the Holy Spirit makes intercession for the saints [according to Bible language, this means all believers] according to the will of God. So, when we pray in our prayer language the Holy Ghost gives us the words to say to direct our prayers according to His wisdom.

Suppose I said to you that I know someone who desires to be your prayer partner. This person is available anytime, night or day. It is a person who knows you better than you know yourself and knows exactly how to pray in a way that is best for you. And best of all, this person's prayers are ALWAYS answered. Are you interested? Then let me introduce you. Just say "Hello, Holy Spirit".

Begin today to set aside a specific time to "Present your body as a living sacrifice, holy and acceptable to God" (Romans 12:1) [preferably first thing in the morning] and allow the Holy Spirit to use your tongue to pray out His perfect plan for your life. Begin by even 15 minutes a day and watch what happens. Soon it will not be a matter of effort to start, it will be something you do not want to stop.

If you have been born again, and would like to receive

the baptism in the Holy Spirit, pray this prayer.

Heavenly Father, I thank you that I have been born again by the blood of Jesus and counted worthy to receive Him into my life. Please baptize me in your Holy Spirit and enable me to pray in a Heavenly language so that I can yield my tongue to you and pray out your plans for my life and for those for whom you call me to intercede. I want to be totally yielded to you so that in all things in every area of my life your will shall be done. I thank you that you are faithful to do it. That when I ask for the Holy Spirit I will receive Him and nothing else because I ask this through Christ my Lord. AMEN

If you have prayed this prayer, God is faithful who has promised and He will do what He has said He will do. He has promised that whoever asks for the Holy Spirit will receive Him so it is already done. Begin to thank Him and whatever words come to your mouth to say, speak them forth. They may sound funny and strange because it will be a language you don't know. But God is faithful and you can be sure that the words you speak are words that the Holy Spirit has given you to say. Spend some time just worshipping Him and thanking Him for the precious gift of Himself.

Why is the Bible divided into Old and New "Testaments"?

The Hebrew word *ber-eeth'* which is translated "covenant" or "testament" literally means "cutting" or "compact made by passing through the pieces of flesh".

When two persons entered into a covenant in Bible times (and even today in some primitive societies) it works like this:

First, they cut their wrists (notice the word "cutting" in the definition) and they mingle their blood. Then they sacrifice an animal, split it in two parts, and walk between the pieces. Notice how this corresponds to the second part of the definition: "compact made by passing through the pieces of flesh". They also eat a meal - usually bread and wine or part of the animal sacrifice - they exchange garments, and they exchange names.

All this signifies that from that point on they are one. Everything they each own, they now own in common. For example, if you and I enter into a covenant, everything I have is yours, and everything you have is mine. You don't need to ask for anything you want from me. You just have to take it. It is already yours. Also, if you are attacked, I will defend you. And you do the same for me. More simply put, it means we "belong to" one another. I belong to you and you belong to me. Covenant also continues to our descendents. In other words, what I have belongs to your children also, and your children's children, and so on, so death doesn't break the covenant. But if one does break a covenant, it is punishable by death.

Once we get a basic understanding of covenant the entire Bible begins to make sense. Covenant is the concept around which the Bible and, indeed, God's relationship with man on earth, is established.

It is interesting to note that marriage is a blood covenant. God uses the term "marriage" to describe His relationship with Israel (Isaiah 54:5) and Christ's relationship with the Church. (Revelation 21:9, 22:17)

To understand covenant, we first have to understand that when God speaks, it is. In other when God says anything, it becomes a law. Like the law of gravity, it cannot change. God never changes and what He says remains forever unchanged.

Forever, O LORD, thy word is settled in heaven. (Psalm 119:89)

When God created Adam in the garden, He gave him dominion over all the earth.

And God said, Let us make man in our image, after our likeness: and let them have dominion over the fish of the sea, and over the fowl of the air, and over the cattle, and over all the earth, and over every creeping thing that creepeth upon the earth. (Genesis 1:26)

This dominion is only for a set time, the end of which the prophet Daniel refers to when he speaks of the "end of days". (Daniel 12:13) Jesus also referred to the end of this time.

So shall it be at the end of the world: the angels shall come forth, and sever the wicked from among the just, (Matthew 13:49)

The Greek word *ahee-ohn'* translated as "world" is more correctly translated "age". So, Jesus is speaking of the end of the Age, or Dispensation.

God created man as a being with free will to choose whom he would serve in order to have a creature who would serve Him willingly from love, by choice, not blindly out of ignorance or by coercion. So, Adam had a choice.

The Bible tells us whomever we obey becomes our master, and we become their servant.

Know ye not, that to whom ye yield yourselves servants to obey, his servants ye are to whom ye obey; whether of sin unto death, or of obedience unto righteousness? (Romans 6:16)

So when Satan came into the garden in the form of a serpent and tempted Adam and Eve to disobey God and they yielded to him and did so (Genesis 3:1-7), Satan became their master. By doing so, they transferred their God-given authority to Satan. But God knew that this would happen. Before the "foundation of the world" (Revelation 13:8) God had a plan for the salvation of mankind. This plan was "covenant".

Since God had given dominion to man He could not do

anything on this earth without man's permission. Notice I said "could not", not "would not". You say, "But He is God, He can do anything".

No, God cannot do everything. There are at least two things that God cannot do. God cannot lie, and God cannot break His word. Why? Because once He says something, it is so. He doesn't just *tell* the truth. He IS truth. Jesus said, *"I am the way, the truth, and the life".* (John 14:6)

Therefore, because God had given dominion to man, he found a man who would make a covenant with Him so that he could legally, according to the law He had spoken by his own mouth, intervene on the earth.

This man was Abraham.

And when Abram was ninety years old and nine, the LORD appeared to Abram, and said unto him, I am the Almighty God; walk before me, and be thou perfect.
And I will make my covenant between me and thee, and will multiply thee exceedingly.. (Genesis 17:1, 2)

God told Abraham to sacrifice some animals, split them in two, divide the pieces, and lay them on the ground. (Genesis 15:9, 10)

He then put Abraham into a deep sleep and the Bible tells us:

And it came to pass, that, when the sun went down, and it was dark, behold a smoking furnace, and a burning

lamp that passed between those pieces.
(Genesis 15:17)

God Himself walked between the pieces, signifying that Abraham had nothing to bring to this covenant, everything he had God had given him, but God is saying, "Everything I have is yours".
They exchanged names. From that time on God was known as "the God of Abraham". (He still is!) and God changed Abraham's name from Abram to Abraham.

Neither shall thy name any more be called Abram, but
   thy name shall be Abraham; for a father of many
   nations have I made thee. (Genesis 17:5)

The Hebrew letter ה added to Abraham's name to change it from Abram to Abraham is the same letter which appears twice in the Hebrew name for God יהוה (Note: Hebrew is read from right to left.) So, the letter ה is taken from God's name and put into Abraham's name. Jewish tradition associates this letter being used in a person's name as acknowledgement of God. So, in a manner of speaking, God and Abraham exchanged names.

The application of the other covenant conditions will become clear as we go on.

We read much later that God did in fact give Abraham a son. That son was Isaac. (Genesis 21:2, 3) There is a story about Abraham offering Isaac as a sacrifice to God, with which many people are familiar even if they don't know much else about the Bible.

And he (God) said, Take now thy son, thine only son Isaac, whom thou lovest, and get thee into the land of Moriah; and offer him there for a burnt offering upon one of the mountains which I will tell thee of.

And Abraham rose up early in the morning, saddled his ass, took two of his young men with him, and Isaac his son, cleaved the wood for the burnt offering, rose up, and went unto the place of which God had told him.

Then on the third day, Abraham lifted up his eyes, and saw the place afar off.

And Abraham said unto his young men, Abide ye here with the ass; and I and the lad will go yonder and worship, and come again to you.

And Abraham took the wood of the burnt offering, and laid it upon Isaac his son; and he took the fire in his hand, and a knife; and they went both of them together.

And Isaac spoke unto Abraham his father, and said, My father: and he said, Here am I, my son. And he said, Behold the fire and the wood: but where is the lamb for a burnt offering?

And Abraham said, My son, God will provide himself a lamb for a burnt offering: so they went both of them together.

And they came to the place which God had told him of; and Abraham built an altar there, and laid the wood in order, and bound Isaac his son, and laid him on the altar upon the wood.

And Abraham stretched forth his hand, and took the knife to slay his son.

And the angel of the LORD called unto him out of heaven, and said, Abraham, Abraham: and he said, Here am I.

And he said, Lay not thine hand upon the lad, neither
do thou any thing unto him: for now I know that
thou fearest God, seeing thou hast not withheld thy
son, thine only son from me.
And Abraham lifted up his eyes, and looked, and behold
behind him a ram caught in a thicket by his horns:
and Abraham went and took the ram, and offered
him up for a burnt offering in the stead of his son.
(Genesis 22:2-13)

Let's reiterate what we have read. God called Isaac to go to the land of Moriah and offer Isaac as a sacrifice to God. So, Abraham obeyed God and did everything God told Him to do. When Abraham demonstrated that he was fully prepared to sacrifice His son for God, God sent an angel to stop him from going through with it and sent a ram to be the sacrifice. Because he was willing, God counted it to him as if he had done it.

"...for now I know that thou fearest God, seeing thou
hast not withheld thy son, thine only son from me."
(Genesis 2:12)

Even though Abraham did not go through with his intention to sacrifice Isaac, God counted it as though he had.

For if there be first a willing mind, it is accepted
according to that a man hath, and not according to that
he hath not. (II Corinthians 8:12)

Unless we understand covenant, this story makes no sense whatsoever. But when we understand that because God had given dominion to man it was *necessary* for a man to covenant with God and offer his son as a sacrifice to God before God could offer His son to man as a sacrifice for man. This was the institution of the "Old Covenant" which was to Abraham and his offspring, Isaac, and Jacob, (whose name God later changed to Israel) and, ultimately, the Jewish people and the nation of Israel.

The Bible is speaking of this in this passage:

Be ye mindful always of his covenant; the word that he commanded to a thousand generations;
Even of the covenant that he made with Abraham, and of his oath unto Isaac;
And hath confirmed the same to Jacob for a law, and to Israel for an everlasting covenant, (I Chronicles 16:15)

Notice it says that this covenant is commanded for "a thousand generations" and it is also referred to as an "everlasting covenant".

We also need to understand that the "law" or "commandments" were given to Moses because he was a descendant of Abraham and therefore under the Abrahamic covenant. They were given to outline the means by which the people were to live under the covenant in order to appropriate the blessings of God, which belonged to them through the covenant. The first five books of the Bible, referred to as the "Torah" are primarily a description and outline of the old covenant.

This is an extremely brief explanation of covenant and there have been many books written on this subject.

But it is essential to have some understanding of the concept of covenant to understand the Bible at all.

> *And the angel of the LORD called unto Abraham out of heaven the second time, And said, By myself have I sworn, saith the LORD, for because thou hast done this thing, and hast not withheld thy son, thine only son:*
> *That in blessing I will bless thee, and in multiplying I will multiply thy seed as the stars of the heaven, and as the sand which is upon the sea shore; and thy seed shall possess the gate of his enemies;*
> *And in thy seed shall all the nations of the earth be blessed; because thou hast obeyed my voice.*
> (Genesis 22:15-18)

Since Abraham, a man, offered Isaac as a sacrifice to God, under the conditions of covenant, the way had now been made for God to send His son Jesus "in the fullness of time" to be a sacrifice for all mankind. The "seed" of Abraham referred to in verse 18 above in which "all the nations of the earth [shall] be blessed" is Jesus. When you trace the genealogy of Jesus, in Matthew 1:1-16, you find that he was descended from Abraham, or He was Abraham's "seed".

But when the fullness of the time was come, God sent forth his Son, made of a woman, made under the law, (Galatians 4:4)

God spoke through the prophet Jeremiah spoke of a "new covenant" which was yet to come.

Behold, the days come, saith the LORD, that I will

make a new covenant with the house of Israel, and
with the house of Judah: (Jeremiah 31:31)

In the old covenant there were commandments given by which men should live in order to stay under the protection of God and receive His provision and blessing. When the law was broken, it was punishable by death. Remember we said the penalty of breaking covenant is death. But God provided an "atonement" for breaking the commandment [sin]. The atonement in the old covenant was an animal. The animal became a substitute to take the penalty for sin. The blood of an animal was shed and if the sacrifice of the animal was accepted by God, fire came down from heaven and consumed the sacrifice on the alter.

Now when Solomon had made an end of praying, the
fire came down from heaven, and consumed the burnt
offering and the sacrifices; and the glory of the LORD
filled the house. (II Chronicles 7:1)

The blood of animals provided an atonement for sin - a substitute or a "covering" for sin. In the old covenant, once a year the priest would offer the sacrifice for sin. It was the atonement for the sin's of the people for one year. When Jesus died on the cross, He became the final sacrifice. He made the way for us to come into a "new and better covenant".

The Bible tells us this in the Book of Hebrews:

But now hath he obtained a more excellent ministry, by
how much also he is the mediator of a better covenant,
which was established upon better promises.
(Hebrews 8:6)

It explains that when the sacrifice was offered each year for sins there was a "remembrance" of sin. In other words, the sin was "remembered" it wasn't forgotten. They were just no longer required to pay the penalty, because the penalty was substitutionally passed onto the animals.

But when Jesus became our "sacrifice" for sin, there is no longer a remembrance of sin, it has become "remitted". To "remit" means to do away with. If you owe a bill and it has been remitted, if you try to pay the bill after it has been remitted, you will be told, "You don't owe that anymore, there is no need to pay". It is no longer remembered. It is as if it never was.

The writer to the Hebrews says here about the new covenant:

By the which will we are sanctified through the offering of the body of Jesus Christ once for all.
And every priest standeth daily ministering and offering oftentimes the same sacrifices, which can never take away sins:
But this man, after he had offered one sacrifice for sins forever, sat down on the right hand of God; (Hebrews 10:10-12)

He is saying that Jesus offered his body once, forever, for all mankind and "sat down on the right hand of God", signifying the work was done.

Recall, when He died on the cross the last words He spoke were *"It is finished".* (John 19:30)

These were the most powerful words ever uttered in the Universe since God spoke the words "Let there be light".

Jesus is saying by the words "It is finished" that He has completed the plan for the redemption of man from the sin of Adam. He has paid the penalty in full for the sin of every man who ever lived and redeemed each of us from the curse of that sin. He has totally fulfilled all the law on our behalf. He has fulfilled our side of the covenant for us.

Think not that I am come to destroy the law, or the prophets: I am not come to destroy, but to fulfil. (Matthew 5:17)

All we need to do - all we can do - is receive.

We do not earn God's redemption; we only receive. We receive by faith, by believing that Jesus is who He is and that He has done what He has done.
For God so loved the world, that he gave his only begotten Son, that whosoever believeth in him should not perish, but have everlasting life. (John 3:16)

In the old covenant, the people of God were called "servants" of God.

For unto me the children of Israel are servants; they are my servants whom I brought forth out of the land of Egypt: I am the LORD your God. (Leviticus 25:55)
In the new covenant, we are the "sons of God".

For ye have not received the spirit of bondage
*   again to fear; but ye have received the Spirit of*
*   adoption, where by we cry, Abba, Father.*
*   The Spirit itself beareth witness with our spirit, that*
*   we are the children of God:*   (Romans 8:15,16)

Beloved, now are we the sons of God, (I John 3:2)

We have seen the picture that covenant is an exchange.
One exchanges garments, one exchanges names, one
basically exchanges everything one owns. Let us look
at the "exchange" which takes place when we enter into
the new covenant through faith in Jesus Christ.

The first thing we exchange is our sin for His
righteousness.

For he [God] hath made him [Jesus] to be sin for us,
*   who knew no sin; that we might be made the*
*   righteousness of God in him.* (II Corinthians 5:21)
Notice it says that Jesus "became" sin so that we might
"become" the **righteousness of God** in Him.

Secondly, we see He took our sickness to give us
healing.

Surely he hath borne our griefs, and carried our
*   sorrows: yet we did esteem him stricken, smitten of*
*   God, and afflicted.*
But he was wounded for our transgressions, he was
*   bruised for our iniquities: the chastisement of our*
*   peace was upon him; and with his stripes we are*
*   healed.*   (Isaiah 53:4, 5)

This is one of the most significant passages in the Bible

prophetic of Jesus. The Hebrew word here *khol-ee'* which is translated "griefs" is more accurately translated "disease" or "sickness". And the Hebrew word *mak-obe'* and translated "sorrows" can also be translated as "pains". Both of these words are translated differently in the New Testament.

When the even was come, they brought unto him many
  that were possessed with devils: and he cast out the
  spirits with his word, and healed all that were sick:
That it might be fulfilled which was spoken by Isaiah
  the prophet, saying, Himself took our infirmities,
  and bare our sicknesses. (Matthew 8:16,17)

Notice the last verse. "Himself took our infirmities, and bare our sicknesses". The words translated as "griefs" and "sorrows" in Isaiah are translated as "infirmities" and "sicknesses" here. And recall from Isaiah 53:4 "and by his stripes we were healed". Again, notice He took **our** infirmities and **our** sicknesses!

So, we exchange our sickness for his healing. Healing belongs to us.

Thirdly, we exchange our poverty for his wealth.

For ye know the grace of our Lord Jesus Christ, that,
  though he was rich, yet for your sakes he became
  poor, that ye through his poverty might be rich.
  (II Corinthians 8:9)

This verse makes it very clear that He took our poverty to give us abundant provision.

Even in the Old Covenant, prosperity was a provision.

Let's examine the blessings that resulted from the old covenant.

Blessed shalt thou be in the city, and blessed shalt thou be in the field.

Blessed shall be the fruit of thy body, and the fruit of thy ground, and the fruit of thy cattle, the increase of thy kine, and the flocks of thy sheep.

Blessed shall be thy basket and thy store.

Blessed shalt thou be when thou comest in, and blessed shalt thou be when thou goest out.

The LORD shall cause thine enemies that rise up against thee to be smitten before thy face: they shall come out against thee one way, and flee before thee seven ways.

The LORD shall command the blessing upon thee in thy storehouses, and in all that thou settest thine hand unto; and he shall bless thee in the land which the LORD thy God giveth thee.

The LORD shall establish thee a holy people unto himself, as he hath sworn unto thee, if thou shalt keep the commandments of the LORD thy God, and walk in his ways.

And all people of the earth shall see that thou art called by the name of the LORD; and they shall be afraid of thee.

And the LORD shall make thee plenteous in goods, in the fruit of thy body, and in the fruit of thy cattle, and in the fruit of thy ground, in the land which the LORD swore unto thy fathers to give thee.

The LORD shall open unto thee his good treasure, the heaven to give the rain unto thy land in his season, and to bless all the work of thine hand: and thou shalt lend unto many nations, and thou shalt not borrow.

And the LORD shall make thee the head, and not the tail; and thou shalt be above only, and thou shalt not be beneath; if that thou hearken unto the commandments of the LORD thy God, which I command thee this day, to observe and to do them: (Deuteronomy 28:3-13)

This is a picture of abundant blessing - health, protection, and prosperity.

And ours is a "better covenant" than this one.

But now hath he (Jesus) *obtained a more excellent ministry, by how much also he is the mediator of a <u>better covenant</u>, which was established upon better promises.* (Hebrews 8:6)

This passage is speaking of the fact that Jesus is mediator of the new covenant, which is a "better covenant" than the old. If God made the people under the old covenant "plenteous in goods", how much more will he provide for us under the new and better covenant.

Again, we are told by Paul in the letter to the Philippians,

But my God shall supply all your need according to his riches in glory by Christ Jesus. (Philippians 4:19)

So, prosperity belongs to us.

Finally, and, most important of all, He took our death to

give us eternal life.

But we see Jesus, who was made a little lower than the angels for the suffering of death, crowned with glory and honor; that he by the grace of God should taste death for every man. (Hebrews 2:9)

And Jesus is speaking of this transfer here, because we appropriate the promises of this covenant by faith.

Verily, verily, I say unto you, He that heareth my word, and believeth on him that sent me, hath everlasting life, and shall not come into condemnation; but is passed from death unto life. (John 5:24)

Through Jesus' death, we have passed from death to eternal life.

Recall that in covenant we exchange names. This is why we are known as "Christians" and this is why we can now claim this promise:

And whatsoever ye shall ask in my name, that will I do, that the Father may be glorified in the Son.
(John 14:13)

And again:

And these signs shall follow them that believe; In my name shall they cast out devils; they shall speak with new tongues;
They shall take up serpents; and if they drink any deadly thing, it shall not hurt them; they shall lay hands on the sick, and they shall recover.
(Mark 16:17,18)

Understanding covenant is essential to understanding

why we pray "in the Name of Jesus".

The final thing we must remember in order to appropriate the blessings which God has already freely bestowed upon us through Christ. Covenant is a two-way commitment. If everything God has is mine, all I have and all that am belongs to Him.

The apostle Paul put it this way:

I am crucified with Christ: nevertheless I live; yet not I, but Christ liveth in me: and the life which I now live in the flesh I live by the faith of the Son of God, who loved me, and gave himself for me. (Galatians 2:20)

Obedience is the way we receive our inheritance in Christ.

The Bible tells us,

And whatsoever we ask, we receive of him, because we keep his commandments, and do those things that are pleasing in his sight. (I John 3:22)

When we are failing to see the answers to our prayers that the Word tells us should be ours, we have to examine ourselves and see if we are failing to obey Him in any way. And in order to know His will we must know His Word.

The Word is the documentation of God's covenant with us. It is a legal document. It is the document on which our own legal system is based. The word "testament" is a legal term. It is a legal document that outlines actions to be taken after a person's death and the distribution of the testator's property and effects. Jesus died on the cross to institute the New Testament. It outlines God's will to us - His "last will and testament. We are heirs to everything Jesus had on this earth.

The Spirit itself beareth witness with our spirit, that we are the children of God:
And if children, then heirs; heirs of God, and joint-heirs with Christ; (Romans 8:16,17)

But to know what is ours, we must know the Word.

It is important in reading the Word to remember whom God is talking to in each section. The Old Testament is written to the Jews under the old covenant. The gospels are an account of Jesus ministering to Jews under the old covenant and of His atoning sacrifice fulfilling the old covenant and thereby instituting the new covenant. The remainder of the New Testament - the book of Acts, the epistles and the book of Revelation - are written to Christians under the new covenant.

When you read the Bible in the light of this understanding, it will make more sense.

The most powerful passage referring to what Jesus did for us on the cross is found in Revelation 5.

And I beheld, and I heard the voice of many angels round about the throne and the beasts and the elders: and the number of them was ten thousand times ten thousand, and thousands of thousands;

Saying with a loud voice, Worthy is the Lamb that was slain to receive power, and riches, and wisdom, and strength, and honour, and glory, and blessing. (Revelation 5:11, 12)

But Jesus had all these things to begin with. Why should He need to "receive" them?

The answer is found in the following passages.

And if ye be Christ's, then are ye Abraham's seed, and heirs according to the promise. (Galatians 3:29)

The Spirit itself beareth witness with our spirit, that we are the children of God:
And if children, then heirs; heirs of God, and joint-heirs with Christ; if so be that we suffer with him, that we may be also glorified together. (Romans 8:16)

We see from this passage that He received all these things in order that we might receive with Him. As "joint heirs", what He receives, we receive. He received them for us.

Meditate on these passages until what Jesus has done for you, and what you are and have in Him is more real than your temporal circumstances, so that you may build the faith to receive and walk in everything He has done for you.

My prayer for everyone who reads this chapter is that you will be brought into a deeper level of understanding the awesome greatness of our Heavenly Father, His unsearchable love for us in sending His son to redeem us and the unfathomable riches of His Glory which are ours as the result of the unspeakable gift of His atoning sacrificial death on the cross.

What is Communion?

When God made the covenant with Abraham, he prophesied to him that his descendents would be slaves in a strange land for four hundred years.

And he said unto Abram, Know of a surety that thy seed shall be a stranger in a land that is not theirs, and shall serve them; and they shall afflict them four hundred years; (Genesis 15:13)

That land was Egypt.

When Joseph (son of Jacob, [whose name God changed to Israel], son of Abraham) was sold into slavery by his brothers, (Genesis 37) he ended up in Egypt where he became second in command to Pharaoh (Genesis 41). There came a great famine in the land and Joseph's family came to Egypt to find food. They then remained for four hundred years. After Joseph's death another Pharaoh arose who didn't favor Israel and the descendents of Israel became slaves in the land.

After four hundred years God raised up Moses to deliver his people from the Egyptians. (Exodus 1) Pharaoh refused to allow the Israelites to leave Egypt until God intervened with miracles and plagues. (Exodus 7,8,9,10) At last, the Pharaoh told the Israelites they could leave Egypt. The night before they left Egypt, God commanded them to sacrifice a lamb for each household. They were to eat a meal with the flesh of the lamb, unleavened bread and bitter herbs. They were to take the blood of the lamb and apply it to the side posts and the upper doorpost of the houses. God was going to send an angel through the land and kill every firstborn in the land of Egypt, both man and beast, and execute judgment on the land of Egypt. When the angel of death saw the blood on the doorposts he would "passover" their house. This feast was called "the Lord's Passover" and the Jewish people continue to observe it to this day.

When Jesus came to become our savior and redeemer, He became the Passover or "Pascal" lamb. He fulfilled this feast for the whole world, for whosoever would believe on Him.

On the night before He was crucified He was gathered with His disciples celebrating the feast of Passover.

And he took bread, and gave thanks, and broke it, and gave unto them, saying, This is my body which is given for you: this do in remembrance of me.
Likewise also the cup after supper, saying, This cup is the new testament in my blood, which is shed for you. (Luke 22:19,20)

The Jews also celebrated the Sabbath with a meal of bread and wine. Christians began to celebrate the Sabbath with bread and wine in remembrance of Christ and His last supper, as He said "Do this in remembrance of me".

Let's examine this passage of scripture.

Then Jesus said unto them, "Verily, verily, I say unto you, Except ye eat the flesh of the Son of man, and drink his blood, ye have no life in you.

Whoso eateth my flesh, and drinketh my blood, hath eternal life; and I will raise him up at the last day.

For my flesh is meat indeed, and my blood is drink indeed.

He that eateth my flesh, and drinketh my blood, dwelleth in me, and I in him.

As the living Father hath sent me, and I live by the Father: so he that eateth me, even he shall live by me.

This is that bread which came down from heaven: not as your fathers did eat manna, and are dead: he that eateth of this bread shall live forever." (John 6:53-58)

Jesus said that unless we "eat His flesh" and "drink His blood" we have no life in us. How do we "eat the flesh" and "drink the blood" of Jesus? By taking the wine and bread of communion as the Body and Blood of Christ.

There is another scriptural type of Jesus as the "Bread of Life" in the Old Testament. When the "children of Israel" had been led out of Egypt by Moses they "wandered in the wilderness" (Joshua 14:10) for forty years. From the place where they crossed the Red Sea and left Egypt, to the place where they crossed the Jordan River to enter into the Promised Land, was approximately an eleven-day march. But they were led by God (not knowing the way) in circles in the "wilderness" or desert for forty years until they had finally learned to walk in the obedience and faith they needed to survive in the "promised land" where there were enemies they would need God's help to resist.

While they were in the wilderness God fed them supernaturally with a type of bread which they called "manna" (the Hebrew word *mawn* which means literally "whatness" or "what is it?") because they didn't know what it was. They had to go out each day, first thing in the morning and gather the manna. They were to gather just enough for one day, no more. If they tried to save it, it would rot.

And when the dew that lay was gone up, behold, upon the face of the wilderness there lay a small round thing, as small as the hoar frost on the ground.

And when the children of Israel saw it, they said one to another, It is manna: for they knew not what it was. And Moses said unto them, This is the bread which the LORD hath given you to eat.

This is the thing which the LORD hath commanded, Gather of it every man according to his eating, an omer for every man, according to the number of your persons; take ye every man for them which are in his tents.

And the children of Israel did so, and gathered, some more, some less.

And when they did mete it with an omer, he that gathered much had nothing over, and he that gathered little had no lack; they gathered every man according to his eating.

And Moses said, Let no man leave of it till the morning.

Notwithstanding they hearkened not unto Moses; but some of them left of it until the morning, and it bred worms, and stank: and Moses was wroth with them.
(Exodus 16:14:21)

They could eat it raw, or cook it various ways. On the

day before the Sabbath (Friday, since Saturday is the Jewish Sabbath) they were to gather twice as much as on the other days, because they were commanded to honor the Sabbath (seventh) day and keep it holy unto God. So, they were not to gather any on the Sabbath, as they were not to do any work on the Sabbath.

And they gathered it every morning, every man according to his eating: and when the sun waxed hot, it melted.

And it came to pass, that on the sixth day they gathered twice as much bread, two omers for one man: and all the rulers of the congregation came and told Moses.

And he said unto them, This is that which the LORD hath said, Tomorrow is the rest of the holy sabbath unto the LORD: bake that which ye will bake today, and seethe that ye will seethe; and that which remaineth over lay up for you to be kept until the morning.

And they laid it up till the morning, as Moses bade: and it did not stink, neither was there any worm therein.

And Moses said, Eat that today; for today is a sabbath unto the LORD: today ye shall not find it in the field.

Six days ye shall gather it; but on the seventh day, which is the sabbath, in it there shall be none.

And it came to pass, that there went out some of the people on the seventh day for to gather, and they found none. (Exodus 16:22-27)

This is the "bread" Jesus was referring to in the following passage:

*Our fathers did eat manna in the desert; as it is written,
He gave them bread from heaven to eat.*

*Then Jesus said unto them, "Verily, verily, I say unto
you, Moses gave you not that bread from heaven;
but my Father giveth you the true bread from
heaven.*

*For the bread of God is he which cometh down from
heaven, and giveth life unto the world."*

*Then said they unto him, Lord, evermore give us this
bread.*

*And Jesus said unto them, "I am the bread of life: he
that cometh to me shall never hunger; and he that
believeth on me shall never thirst."*   (John
6:31,35)

The Old Covenant was given as a picture, or foreshadowing, of what is fulfilled in Jesus. To totally understand what it means to be a Christian, we need to understand the Old Testament. They are connected.

It has been said that the New Testament is revealed in the Old Testament and the Old Testament is fulfilled in the New Testament.

When we take communion, we take wine and bread, just as the Jewish people do when they celebrate Shabbat and Passover, and we ask God to bless it. We ask Him to let it become for us the Body and Blood of Christ, and we partake of it as an act of worship. It is far more than just a ritual; it is a celebration of our "oneness" in Him. Of His faithfulness and goodness and the precious price He paid when He sent His son to die for us. It is an act of thanksgiving to Jesus for becoming our sacrifice and loving us just as we are.

And it is a renewal of our commitment to present our bodies to Him as a "living sacrifice". (Romans 12:1) It is our "covenant meal".

What is worship?

Worship is the single most important concept pertaining to Christianity. If you can get hold of this, not just intellectually, but realize and live it, everything else will follow.

We were created to worship. We were created to have a connected, living, breathing relationship with the Father of Life. We were created to "live and move and have our being" in Him. And through that relationship, everything we need is provided. Everything. Nothing lacking, nothing missing. When God looked on His creation in the "Garden of Eden", the Bible tells us "it was good".

And God saw every thing that he had made, and, behold, it was very good. And the evening and the morning were the sixth day. (Genesis 1:31)

It says that every thing that God had made was very good. What happened?

Earth was created for man. Man was created to function in the presence of God, having fellowship with Him, loving Him, and tending the creation God had given him in the wisdom derived from fellowshipping daily with God and learning from Him. Through that relationship with God everything he needed was provided - food, water, healing, peace, joy, contentment, love – nothing lacking, nothing missing.

When Adam and Eve sinned (disobeyed God) that

fellowship was broken. That divine connection to Goodness, Wisdom and Truth was severed.

Man is created to be divinely connected to God. Worship is that connection

If you buy a computer, you take it home and connect it to an electrical outlet. If you do not plug it in, it won't work. It is that simple. It was designed to operate on electrical energy, and without an energy source, it won't work. If you go overseas, you may connect it to another kind of energy source. It will not function properly. You may buy a battery pack. It will function for a while, but eventually the battery pack has to be charged from the same type of source the computer was originally designed to use. It is only by being connected to the type of power source that it was designed to use that it will function properly for the entire time it is able to function at all.

This is a very crude example. But you were designed to be connected to God. He is your creator and sustainer. If you are not rightly connected to Him, it creates a void. You will attempt to fill that void with other things. Whatever it is, you will become overly attached to it. It may be cigarettes, alcohol or sex. It may be things that are good in themselves, food, work, sports, television, the Internet – (Hello!). Sometimes it is a particular kind of attitude, perfectionism, over-attention to small details, routine - a compulsion to have everything in its place and do everything at a specific time in a specific way, etc. But, whatever it is, it will upset the balance of your life and it will never bring you the peace and joy you are longing for. Something will always be missing.

The Bible tells us that in God's presence is "fullness of joy".

Thou wilt show me the path of life: in thy presence is fullness of joy; at thy right hand there are pleasures forevermore. (Psalms 16:11)

To have "fullness of joy" is to be filled with joy. That is all the joy you can contain. You cannot have any more joy than that!

Your spirit man knows this. The Bible tells us every creature has knowledge of the Creator.

For the invisible things of him from the creation of the world are clearly seen, being understood by the things that are made, even his eternal power and Godhead; so that they are without excuse:
Because that, when they knew God, they glorified him not as God, neither were thankful; but became vain in their imaginations, and their foolish heart was darkened. (Romans 1:19-21)

From the time we are sent from God's presence into this world, (Ecclesiastes 12:7) our spirits have a yearning for Him that only He can fill. When we do not allow Him to fill us, we create a lack of joy, a lack of contentment, a lack of ease - "dis-ease", if you will. We try to recapture that joy by any other means that are available to us. They seem to offer a diversion, at first. They distract us from the longing. They amuse us. But after a time the novelty wears off and they bore us. We then either turn to something else, or go after the same thing to a greater extent. We reason it worked the first time, maybe if I just do it more it will work again. Sometimes it does. Then, sadly, in many instances, we find we can't stop.

Man is "addictive" by nature. We were created to be "addicted" to God.

King David said,

As the hart panteth after the water brooks, so panteth my soul after thee, O God. (Psalm 42:1)

My soul longeth, yea even fainteth for the courts of the LORD: my heart and my flesh crieth out for the living God. (Psalm 84:2)

We were created to be consumed with love for God.

For the LORD thy God is a consuming fire, even a jealous God. (Deuteronomy 4:24)

But we are very fickle, unstable people.

In the wilderness when Moses was on the mountain receiving the commandments from God, the children of Israel got impatient and restless. Moses had been their connection to God and he had been on the mountain forty days. They did what children without supervision do; they got into trouble. They gathered all their gold, made a golden calf, and bowed down to worship it.

Man *will* worship something.

We were created to worship. Everyone worships something. Your character, the person you are, is determined by what you worship. It is the amount of time you spend pursuing the things in your life which will demonstrate what you worship. Examine what it is which receives most of your time and energy. This is what you value most. This is your god.

God knows this. It is He who created us this way. This is the reason He gave the laws in the old covenant.

In the Old Testament there were extensive and exhaustive commandments given pertaining to worship. There were detailed commandments given as to the construction of the tabernacle, the rituals to be conducted in the tabernacle, the sanctification of the priests and every item that was used in the tabernacle. Then there were commandments given pertaining to every aspect of daily life. God gave provision for every area of life in the Torah, the first five books of the Old Testament.

Worship in the Old Covenant consisted of an outward expression. It was all-pervasive and affected every aspect of life, but it was still confined to an outward expression. It was designed to be a constant external reminder of man's dependence on God. Every act, word and attitude had a commandment pertaining to it to keep the people connected to God and in the path of His blessing and provision. These commandments were given to Moses on Mount Sinai and written on tablets of stone.

But God prophesied through Jeremiah that He would make a new covenant, where His laws would be written on the hearts of men, not on tablets of stone.

Behold, the days come, saith the LORD, that I will make a new covenant with the house of Israel, and with the house of Judah:

Not according to the covenant that I made with their fathers in the day that I took them by the hand to bring them out of the land of Egypt; which my covenant they broke, although I was a husband unto them, saith the LORD:

But this shall be the covenant that I will make with the house of Israel; After those days, saith the LORD, I will put my law in their inward parts, and write it in their hearts; and will be their God, and they shall be my people. (Jeremiah 31:31-33)

Jesus referred to New Covenant worship when He told the Samaritan woman,

"But the hour cometh, and now is, when the true worshipers shall worship the Father in spirit and in truth: for the Father seeketh such to worship him." (John 4:23)

In the wilderness, when the Old Covenant worship was instituted, God dwelt in the Tabernacle. He appeared there as a pillar of cloud by day and a pillar of fire by night.

He took not away the pillar of the cloud by day, nor the pillar of fire by night, from before the people.
(Exodus 13:22)

He was physically separate from the people. Only the priests could enter into the Holy of Holies, the innermost chamber of the Tabernacle where God dwelt, and they could enter it only after a ritual purification or sanctification, for which it was necessary to sacrifice animals and apply their blood as atonement for sin, because God is holy and we cannot approach Him with sin. A six-inch thick veil surrounded the Holy of Holies in the temple. When Jesus died on the cross this veil was torn from top to bottom signifying that Jesus had made a way into the Holy of Holies for us.

And, behold, the veil of the temple was rent in twain from the top to the bottom; and the earth did quake, and the rocks rent; (Matthew 27:51)

In the New Covenant, God indwells the hearts of His people. Jesus has become our sacrifice for sin and by His blood has made a way for us into the presence of God once and for all when we receive Him by faith.

In the new covenant, we *are* the temple.

Know ye not that ye are the temple of God, and that the Spirit of God dwelleth in you? (I Corinthians 3:16)

And recall Jesus said,

"If a man love me, he will keep my words: and my Father will love him, and we will come unto him, and make our abode with him." (John 14:23)

To "make one's abode with" is to live with. God lives on the inside of us. This makes us the "temple" of God as we see from I Corinthians 3:16.

God the father, by the Holy Spirit, indwells our spirit. We have access to the same relationship that Adam had in the garden before the fall. But, it is our soul (which consists of our mind, will and emotions) that determines the state of our earthly life and it is our soul that must be renewed daily by our continually choosing the will of God in every area of our lives.

And be not conformed to this world: but be ye transformed by the renewing of your mind, that ye may prove what is that good, and acceptable, and perfect, will of God. (Romans 12:2)

Until we are born again, our soul is ruled by our body. It is our spirit that connects us to God, our soul that connects our spirit to our body, and our body that connects us to the outside world. When we are born again, our spirit is recreated and comes into union with God. At this point we have the choice to allow the Holy Spirit to lead and guide us and empower us to live the life God ordained us to live, or we can choose to continue to allow the world, through what we perceive with our physical senses (our body), to dominate our lives. When we do this, there is very little apparent change in our lives. People who do this are called "carnal", "fleshly", or "worldly" for obvious reasons. In order to appropriate the blessings that belong to us through the covenant God provided us through Jesus we must yield to the Holy Spirit and live according to God's laws, just as they did in the old covenant.

The difference is that whereas the laws of the old covenant were very detailed and complicated, the laws of the new covenant are very simple. Jesus told us,

Thou shalt love the Lord thy God with all thy heart, and with all thy soul, and with all thy mind.
This is the first and great commandment.
And the second is like unto it, Thou shalt love thy neighbor as thyself.
On these two commandments hang all the law and the prophet.." (Matthew 22:37 - 40)

To love the Lord our God, with all our heart, mind and soul is worship. He becomes the very essence of our lives. When we learn to worship Him "in spirit and in truth", we can say with the apostle Paul,

For in him we live, and move, and have our being; as certain also of your own poets have said, [He was talking to the Ephesians] *For we are also his offspring.* (Acts 17:28)

And when we acknowledge His presence in us continually, we allow Him to manifest His love in us and through us, and this love will flow through us to everyone we meet.

And hope maketh not ashamed; because <u>the love of God is shed abroad</u> in our hearts by the Holy Ghost which is given unto us. (Romans 5:5)

The Holy Ghost, who is God, who is love (I John 4:8)

pours his love through us, or it is "shed abroad" through us. We thereby fulfill the second commandment, "Thou shalt love thy neighbor as thyself". And when we love our neighbor as ourselves, we will not kill, steal, lie, or break any of the other commandments regarding how we are to treat others.

Let's look again at the "ten commandments" which are the central commandments of both the Jewish and Christian faith, and upon which our legal system primarily rests.

1. *Thou shalt have none other gods before me.*
2. *Thou shalt not make thee any graven image, or any likeness of any thing that is in heaven above, or that is in the earth beneath, or that is in the waters beneath the earth: Thou shalt not bow down thyself unto them, nor serve them: for I the LORD thy God am a jealous God, visiting the iniquity of the fathers upon the children unto the third and fourth generation of them that hate me,*
3. *Thou shalt not take the name of the LORD thy God in vain: for the LORD will not hold him guiltless that taketh his name in vain.*
4. *Keep the sabbath day to sanctify it, as the LORD thy God hath commanded thee. Six days thou shalt labour, and do all thy work: But the seventh day is the sabbath of the LORD thy God: in it thou shalt not do any work, thou, nor thy son, nor thy daughter, nor thy manservant, nor thy maidservant, nor thine ox, nor thine ass, nor any of thy cattle, nor thy stranger that is within thy gates; that thy manservant and thy maidservant may rest as well as thou.*

5. *Honour thy father and thy mother, as the LORD thy God hath commanded thee; that thy days may be prolonged, and that it may go well with thee, in the land which the LORD thy God giveth thee.*
6. *Thou shalt not kill.*
7. *Neither shalt thou commit adultery.*
8. *Neither shalt thou steal.*
9. *Neither shalt thou bear false witness against thy neighbour.*
10. *Neither shalt thou desire thy neighbour's wife, neither shalt thou covet thy neighbour's house, his field, or his manservant, or his maidservant, his ox, or his ass, or any thing that is thy neighbour's.*
(Deuteronomy 5:7 - 21)

Clearly, if we love the Lord our God with all our heart, mind and soul, and love our neighbor as ourselves, in doing so we will fulfill each of these commandments also.

In the old covenant, the outward obedience to laws of outward behavior directed the consciousness toward God. It worked from the outside in. In the new covenant, the inward intimate relationship with the Father God directs the outward behavior to reflect the indwelling presence of God, (who is Love) on the inside of us. It works from the inside out.

The essence of the Christian walk – please hear this, it is crucial – is <u>learning to keep our focus on God.</u>

When we keep our mind fixed on God, He will keep us in <u>perfect</u> peace.

Thou wilt keep him in perfect peace, whose mind is stayed on thee: because he trusteth in thee. (Isaiah 26:3)

The Hebrew word for peace *sha-lōm,* carries the connotation of total provision for everything necessary for life, total health, total provision, total protection, total joy and total contentment.

When our heart is fixed on God, we will not be afraid of bad news.

He shall not be afraid of evil tidings: his heart is fixed, trusting in the LORD. (Psalms 112:7)

Jesus said,

The light of the body is the eye: if therefore thine eye be single, thy whole body shall be full of light. (Matthew 6:22)

He is saying if our focus is on God, He will light our life. How do we do this?

God gives us clear instruction and example. He uses the example of marriage to illustrate His relationship with us.

For as a young man marrieth a virgin, so shall thy sons marry thee: and as the bridegroom rejoiceth over the bride, so shall thy God rejoice over thee. (Isaiah 62:5)

Again, in the passage we saw earlier:

...which my covenant they broke, although I was a

husband unto them, saith the LORD...
(Jeremiah 31:32)

In a marriage, a husband and wife have a way of attaining intimacy, expressing their love, and expanding their love, that is unique to the marriage relationship (or is supposed to be according to the way God created us). In the Old Testament, the intimacy of a marriage is referred to as "cleaving" together. (Genesis 2:25)

God also commanded his people to "cleave" to Him.

Thou shalt fear the LORD thy God; him shalt thou serve, and to him shalt thou cleave, and swear by his name. (Deuteronomy 10:20)

The Hebrew word *daw-bak'* translated as "cleave" can also be translated to "stick together". Just as in a marriage relationship, in order to develop intimacy, the husband and wife spend time alone with one another, totally and completely concentrating on each other, so we must spend time alone with the Father to develop intimacy with Him. This is the essence of worship.

When we spend time alone with Him, focusing on Him, being absorbed in Him conscious only of Him, His Love and His Glory, we are changed, moment-by-moment into His likeness.

But we all, with open face beholding as in a glass the glory of the Lord, are changed into the same image from glory to glory, even as by the Spirit of the Lord. (II Corinthians 3:18)

It is in our private time with God that we become intimately connected with Him, that we truly come to know Him, and He infuses our nature with His nature, which is Love. Without coming to know Him in this way, we can never truly access His divine plan for our lives, which is a plan of mercy, goodness and love. And in this place of divine connection is everything we need. The Bible refers to this place of intimacy with God as the "secret place" of God.

Read what King David said about the power of remaining in this place with God.

1. *He that dwelleth in the secret place of the most High shall abide under the shadow of the Almighty.*
2. *I will say of the LORD, He is my refuge and my fortress: my God; in him will I trust.*
3. *Surely he shall deliver thee from the snare of the fowler, and from the noisome pestilence.*
4. *He shall cover thee with his feathers, and under his wings shalt thou trust: his truth shall be thy shield and buckler.*
5. *Thou shalt not be afraid for the terror by night; nor for the arrow that flieth by day;*
6. *Nor for the pestilence that walketh in darkness; nor for the destruction that wasteth at noonday.*
7. *A thousand shall fall at thy side, and ten thousand at thy right hand; but it shall not come nigh thee.*
8. *Only with thine eyes shalt thou behold and see the reward of the wicked.*
9. *Because thou hast made the LORD, which is my refuge, even the most High, thy habitation;*
10. *There shall no evil befall thee, neither shall any plague come nigh thy dwelling.*

11.   For he shall give his angels charge over thee, to keep thee in all thy ways.
12.   They shall bear thee up in their hands, lest thou dash thy foot against a stone.
13.   Thou shalt tread upon the lion and adder: the young lion and the dragon shalt thou trample under feet
14.   Because he hath set his love upon me, therefore will I deliver him: I will set him on high, because he hath known my name.
15.   He shall call upon me, and I will answer him: I will be with him in trouble; I will deliver him, and honor him.
16.   With long life will I satisfy him, and show him my salvation. (Psalm 91)

This is a picture of total protection, safety, provision and honor.

When we allow God to assume His rightful place in our lives, He becomes an "all-consuming fire". We become "addicted" to being in His presence, hearing His voice, feeling His touch on our lives. We "hunger and thirst" for His righteousness. When we are wronged, He is the first One we turn to. When we are blessed, our thanks and praise are directed to Him. When we rise in the morning we greet Him, and when we go to bed at night we take an inventory of our day, thank Him for the blessings, ask forgiveness for the failures, cast our care on Him, and go to sleep with the supreme confidence that we are in His hands, loved, protected and secure.

Only you can facilitate this relationship with the Father. He is waiting for you to come. He has been waiting all your life. And He is what you have been longing for. He is the end of all desire. Just come alone with Him to a private place and ask Him to reveal Himself to you and teach you how to love Him, worship Him, serve Him and please Him. You can be assured that He will meet you there, and your life will never be the same.

Why do we need to praise God?

We do not praise God for His benefit, but for ours. The Bible tells us that God created man in His image. There are those who scoffingly say that man created God in his own image. Oddly enough, there is a certain amount of truth in this.

God has given man free will. In order to have a creature who would serve Him by choice, out of love, it was necessary that this be so. So, we have the liberty to serve God, or not to serve God. We have the liberty to believe God, or not believe Him. And we have the liberty to doubt. God will only be to us what we allow Him to be. We can limit Him if we choose.

You ask how can we limit God? The Bible tells us we can limit God by our unbelief. It says of the children of Israel,

How oft did they provoke him in the wilderness, and
grieve him in the desert!
Yea, they turned back and tempted God, and limited the
Holy One of Israel.
(Psalms 78:40,41)

In the New Testament, it tells us that the people in Nazareth limited Jesus.

And when he was come into his own country, he taught
them in their synagogue, insomuch that they
were astonished, and said, Whence hath this
man this wisdom, and these mighty works?

Is not this the carpenter's son? is not his mother called
Mary? and his brethren, James, and Joses, and
Simon, and Judas?
And his sisters, are they not all with us? Whence then
hath this man all these things?
And they were offended in him. But Jesus said unto
them, A prophet is not without honor, save in his
own country, and in his own house.
And he did not many mighty works there because of
their unbelief. (Matthew 13:54-58)

We see here that "he did not many mighty works there
because of their <u>unbelief</u>." They limited Jesus by their
unbelief.

Jesus tells a parable about a noble man who went into a
far country to receive for himself a kingdom, and to
return. And he called ten servants, gave them ten
pounds, and put them in charge until his return. And
when he returned he asked what each had gained by
trading. The first said he had been given ten pounds
and he had gained ten pounds, and the master said
"Well done" and made him ruler over ten cities. The
second said he had been given five pounds and had
gained five pounds, and the master made him ruler over
five cities. The third said, "Here is the pound you gave
me which I have kept hidden in a napkin. I was afraid
of you because you are a hard man; you withdraw what
you didn't deposit and harvest what you didn't plant."
And the master said to him "Out of your own mouth I
will judge you. You knew that I withdraw what I don't
deposit and I harvest what I don't plant, why didn't you
put the money in the bank so it would at least have
gathered interest". And he took from him his pound

and gave it to the one with ten pounds. (Luke 19:12-26)

And another came, saying, Lord, behold, here is thy pound, which I have kept laid up in a napkin: For I feared thee, because thou art an austere man: thou takest up that thou laidst not down, and reapest that thou didst not sow.
And he saith unto him, Out of thine own mouth will I judge thee, thou wicked servant. (Luke 19:20-22)

Notice Jesus said, "Out of thine own mouth will I judge thee".

There is a powerful spiritual principle illustrated here. As the man judged the master to be, the master was to him. The illustration is clear. God can only be to us what we allow Him to be. If we judge Him faithful, He is faithful. He is never unfaithful, but He will not be released to work on our behalf unless we believe Him to be faithful. Believing is faith. He works on our behalf through faith.

Examine the following passages:

But Jesus turned him about, and when he saw her, he said, Daughter, be of good comfort; <u>thy faith hath made thee whole.</u> And the woman was made whole from that hour. (Matthew 9:22)

Then Jesus answered and said unto her, O woman, <u>great is thy faith: be it unto thee even as thou wilt.</u> And her daughter was made whole from that very hour. (Matthew 15:28)

153

When Jesus saw their faith, he said unto the sick of the palsy, Son, thy sins be forgiven thee. (Mark 2:5)
And he said to the woman, Thy faith hath saved thee; go in peace. (Luke 7:50)

And he said unto her, Daughter, be of good comfort: thy faith hath made thee whole; go in peace. (Luke 8:48)

And he said unto him, Arise, go thy way: thy faith hath made thee whole. (Luke 17:19)

And Jesus said unto him, Receive thy sight: thy faith hath saved thee. (Luke 18:42)

In each of these passages, Jesus has said it was the faith of the people receiving (or of others receiving for them) which caused them to receive. Faith is judging God to be merciful, compassionate, able and faithful. Faith for healing is judging God our Healer. Faith for provision is judging God our provider.

What has praise to do with faith? Faith is confidence that God is who He is and that He will intervene in our circumstances.

But without faith it is impossible to please him: for he that cometh to God must believe that he is, and that he is a rewarder of them that diligently seek him. (Hebrews 11:6)

Praise is expressing this confidence in God. It is declaring our righteous judgment of God as our Savior, Healer, Deliver, Provider, Protector, or whatever else we need Him to be.

And as we rightly judge Him to be what He truly is, we release Him to intervene on our behalf.
The Bible tells us "God inhabits our praise". This means when we praise Him, he shows up.

But thou art holy, O thou that inhabitest the praises of Israel. (Psalms 22:3)

So we see God inhabits, or lives in, our praise.

Paul and Silas had been put in jail for preaching the gospel. And the Bible tells us "at the midnight hour" they began to sing praises to God.

And at midnight Paul and Silas prayed, and sang praises unto God: and the prisoners heard them.

And suddenly there was a great earthquake, so that the foundations of the prison were shaken: and immediately all the doors were opened, and every one's bands were loosed.

And the keeper of the prison awaking out of his sleep, and seeing the prison doors open, he drew out his sword, and would have killed himself, supposing that the prisoners had been fled.

But Paul cried with a loud voice, saying, Do thyself no harm: for we are all here.

Then he called for a light, and sprang in, and came trembling, and fell down before Paul and Silas,

And brought them out, and said, Sirs, what must I do to be saved?

And they said, Believe on the Lord Jesus Christ, and thou shalt be saved, and thy house.

And they spake unto him the word of the Lord, and to

all that were in his house.

And he took them the same hour of the night, and washed their stripes; and was baptized, he and all his, straightway. (Acts 16:25-33)

Notice what happened when they began to sing praises. God showed up with an earthquake which broke their bands and opened the prison doors. Then the jailers took them home and washed their wounds, and gave their own lives to Jesus - all because they praised God in the middle of their trouble instead of complaining and grumbling.

Praising God affirms to our hearts Who He really is. It increases our faith. It calls Him on the scene. It releases Him to intervene in our circumstances. It allows Him to be God to us - and it puts the devil to flight!

The following verse tells us how important praise is:

Enter into his gates with thanksgiving, and into his courts with praise: be thankful unto him, and bless his name. (Psalms 100:4)

We see that we come into God's presence with praise. We know that God is always with us, he is everywhere, and once we are born again, he lives inside us. What this means is that His presence becomes manifest. When we praise Him, He allows us to experience that sense of His presence which encourages, empowers, and enriches us in our relationship with Him.

When we praise Him we magnify Him. In other words,

we make Him bigger in our awareness of Him. When we talk about our problems, we magnify them. They become bigger in our awareness. We have to choose daily, moment to moment, what are we going to magnify. When we magnify God, our problems dwindle in His presence and we bring His power on the scene to operate on our behalf to alleviate our problems.

Let's look at another example of the power of praise.

When the Moabites and the Ammonites threatened to come against Judah in battle, Jehoshaphat, King of Judah "set himself to seek God". (II Chronicles 20:3) He proclaimed a fast throughout all Judah and gathered the people together to pray, and here is the prayer he prayed:

O LORD God of our fathers, art not thou God in heaven? and rulest not thou over all the kingdoms of the heathen? and in thine hand is there not power and might, so that none is able to withstand thee?

Art not thou our God, who didst drive out the inhabitants of this land before thy people Israel, and gavest it to the seed of Abraham thy friend forever?

And they dwelt therein, and have built thee a sanctuary therein for thy name, saying,

If, when evil cometh upon us, as the sword, judgment, or pestilence, or famine, we stand before this house, and in thy presence, (for thy name is in this house,) and cry unto thee in our affliction, then thou wilt hear and help.

And now, behold, the children of Ammon and Moab and mount Seir, whom thou wouldest not let Israel invade, when they came out of the land of Egypt, but they turned from them, and destroyed them not;

Behold, I say, how they reward us, to come to cast us out of thy possession, which thou hast given us to inherit.

O our God, wilt thou not judge them? for we have no might against this great company that cometh against us; neither know we what to do: but our eyes are upon thee. (II Chronicles 20:7-12)

Notice He begins by praising God for Who He is and what He has already done, and ends by saying "Our eyes are upon thee". We can learn much from this example.

And God answered Him by saying:

Ye shall not need to fight in this battle: set yourselves, stand ye still, and see the salvation of the LORD with you, O Judah and Jerusalem: fear not, nor be dismayed; tomorrow go out against them: for the LORD will be with you. (II Chronicles 20:17)

Notice God tells them "Fear not". (This phrase occurs 144 times in the Bible. We need to listen!) And He told them they didn't even need to fight, just stand still, the battle was already won, God would win it for them.

The next verse is significant. Notice what they did next.

And Jehoshaphat bowed his head with his face to the ground: and all Judah and the inhabitants of Jerusalem fell before the LORD, worshiping the LORD. (II Chronicles 20:18)

Before the answer came, they worshipped the Lord. We need to worship God before the answer comes. Now notice what Jehoshaphat does next.

And they rose early in the morning, and went forth into the wilderness of Tekoa: and as they went forth, Jehoshaphat stood and said, Hear me, O Judah, and ye inhabitants of Jerusalem; Believe in the LORD your God, so shall ye be established; believe his prophets, so shall ye prosper.
And when he had consulted with the people, he appointed singers unto the LORD, and that should praise the beauty of holiness, as they went out before the army, and to say, Praise the LORD; for his mercy endureth forever. (II Chronicles 20:20,21)

The next day Jehoshaphat appointed <u>praisers</u> to go out before the army. [It is interesting to note that the Hebrew name "Judah" means "to praise".]

Finally, notice what happens as a result of their praise:

And when they began to sing and to praise, the LORD set ambushments against the children of Ammon, Moab, and mount Seir, which were come against Judah; and they were smitten. (II Chronicles 20:22)

When they began to sing to praise, God showed up and defended them. Praise brings God on the scene!

If we can only remember to praise God and magnify Him, He can intervene on our behalf no matter what tries to come against us.

One last thought concerning praise. The Bible tells us praise is "comely".

Rejoice in the LORD, O ye righteous: for praise is comely for the upright. (Psalms 33:1)

Praise ye the LORD: for it is good to sing praises unto our God; for it is pleasant; and praise is comely. (Psalms 147:1)

What does that mean? Miriam-Webster online dictionary defines comely as:

1 : pleasurably conforming to notions of good appearance, suitability, or proportion
2 : having a pleasing appearance; not homely or plain

It also gives "beautiful" as a synonym for "comely". So, in other words, praise looks good on you. It makes you beautiful!

In closing, we need to determine to let praise become a lifestyle. As we praise God, we surround ourselves with His presence and we set ourselves up for His blessing and guidance in our lives. We give him room to intervene in our lives and establish His plans and purposes rather than ours. And He deserves our praise!

What is the "church"?

The Greek word *ekklēsia* translated as "church" in the New Testament means "a calling out" or "the called out ones", in other words, those who have been separated from the rest. The same word is used referring to the children of Israel in Acts 7:38. It refers, in the New Testament to those who have separated themselves unto Christ. It is also referred to as the "Body of Christ". It is the community of believers which is comprised of every person who is "in Christ", or who has been born again. God has brought us to Himself, not just to be united with Him, but also to be united with other believers.

Jesus prayed in the garden before He was crucified that we "all may be one", not only one with Him and the Father, as He and the Father are one, but one with each other.

That they all may be one; as thou, Father, art in me, and I in thee, that they also may be one in us: that the world may believe that thou hast sent me. (John 17:21)

We see by this passage that it is by our relationship with other Christians, as well as by our relationship with Christ, which will be a testimony that Christ has been sent by God.

You were not created to live alone. Once you are born again, you are "in Christ" and thus a "member" of the Body of Christ

Now ye are the body of Christ, and <u>members</u> in particular. (I Corinthians 12:27)

Now therefore ye are no more strangers and foreigners,
*   but fellow citizens with the saints, and of the*
*   household of God;*
And are built upon the foundation of the apostles and
*   prophets, Jesus Christ himself being the chief*
*   corner stone;*
In whom all the building fitly framed together groweth
*   unto a holy temple in the Lord:*
In whom ye also are builded together for a habitation of
God through the Spirit. (Ephesians 2:19,22)

Notice it says you are "builded together". If you are to be "builded together" you need other believers to be "builded together" with.

The "Body of Christ", or the body of believers of Christ, was designed to function as a unit, the strong supporting the weak.

We then that are strong ought to bear the infirmities of the weak, and not to please ourselves. (Romans 15:1)

When we are sick, we are to ask other Christians to pray for us. We are also commanded to pray for each other to help us overcome weakness or temptation.

Is any sick among you? let him call for the elders of the
*   church; and let them pray over him, anointing him*
*   with oil in the name of the Lord:*
And the prayer of faith shall save the sick, and the Lord
*   shall raise him up; and if he have committed sins,*
*   they shall be forgiven him.*

Confess your faults one to another, and pray one for another, that ye may be healed. The effectual fervent prayer of a righteous man availeth much. (James 5:14-16)

Not only do we need the church for prayer for ourselves, but we also need to make ourselves available to pray for others.

In the previous chapter we talked about the importance of personal worship, coming alone to the Father, spending time in His presence and just enjoying Him and meditating on Him and experiencing Who He is and allowing Him to communicate His Heart to us. By now, I hope you have entered in to His presence and begun to experience Him and get a taste of the Glory of Worship and know how indispensable it is in our lives.

When we come together corporately, just to gather in His presence and worship Him together, the presence of God is magnified.

Jesus said,

For where two or three are gathered together in my name, there am I in the midst of them. (Matthew 18:20)

When we gather together with other believers, Jesus has promised He will be in our midst, even if it is only two of us.

When we gather together to pray, there is power in our agreeing together in prayer. Jesus said about this:

Again I say unto you, That if two of you shall agree on earth as touching any thing that they shall ask, it shall be done for them of my Father which is in heaven.
(Matthew 18:19)

The Bible exhorts us to encourage each other:

And let us consider one another to provoke unto love and to good works: Not forsaking the assembling of ourselves together, as the manner of some is; but exhorting one another: and so much the more, as ye see the day approaching. (Hebrews 10:24, 25)

Notice it says, "not forsaking the assembling of ourselves together". It also says we are to exhort, or encourage, one another. We must gather together in order to do this.

We touched briefly on the "gifts of the Holy Spirit" in Chapter 3 when we discussed the Baptism of the Holy Spirit. The gifts of the Holy Spirit were designed to enable the Body of Christ to minister to one another to strengthen, heal, encourage and guide. It is necessary to gather with other believers in order to provide a venue for the Holy Spirit to operate through these gifts so that you may receive ministry from them or so that you may be used to minister them as the Holy Spirit wills. Let's review them briefly:

For to one is given by the Spirit the word of wisdom; to another the word of knowledge by the same Spirit;
To another faith by the same Spirit; to another the gifts of healing by the same Spirit;
To another the working of miracles; to another

166

prophecy; to another discerning of spirits; to another divers kinds of tongues; to another the interpretation of tongues. (I Corinthians 12:8-10)

The Bible also tells us that God has set ministries in the church.

And he gave some, apostles; and some, prophets; and some, evangelists; and some, pastors and teachers;
For the perfecting of the saints, for the work of the ministry, for the edifying of the body of Christ:
Till we all come in the unity of the faith, and of the knowledge of the Son of God, unto a perfect man, unto the measure of the stature of the fullness of Christ:
That we henceforth be no more children, tossed to and fro, and carried about with every wind of doctrine, by the sleight of men, and cunning craftiness, whereby they lie in wait to deceive;
But speaking the truth in love, may grow up into him in all things, which is the head, even Christ:
From whom the whole body fitly joined together and compacted by that which every joint supplieth, according to the effectual working in the measure of every part, maketh increase of the body unto the edifying of itself in love. (Ephesians 4:11-16)

So we see that we need the fellowship of other believers in order to avail ourselves of the ministries – apostles, prophets, evangelists, pastors, and teachers – to be edified and built up in faith, and make ourselves available to ultimately be used by Him in these ministries.

It tells us in verse 16 that the Body of Christ is "fitly joined together" and that the "effectual working in the measure of every part" is necessary for proper function of the body. In other words, each one of us is important in the Body of Christ, and each of us has something to offer. God will use other members of the Body of Christ to help us find our rightful place in Him.

We have already discussed the importance of communion. The Greek word *koy-nohn-ee'-ah* translated as "communion" is also translated as "fellowship". The Bible tells us that we have fellowship with the Father,

That which we have seen and heard declare we unto you, that ye also may have fellowship with us: and truly our fellowship is with the Father, and with his Son Jesus Christ. (I John 1:3)

But it also tells us we have fellowship with each other.

But if we walk in the light, as he is in the light, we have fellowship one with another. (I John 1:7)

Coming together with other believers to celebrate communion strengthens our fellowship both with the father and with other believers.

We have also discussed the importance of baptism. In order to be baptized it is necessary to join with a community of believers who will administer baptism to you.

Finally, God said regarding Adam in the Garden of

Eden "It is not good that man should be alone" (Genesis 2:18) and then He made a wife for him. He has made each of us, male or female, a part of the Body of Christ. We need each other to be complete in Him, to grow in grace and in the power of the Holy Spirit. As you grow in union with Christ and seek Him for direction and guidance, He will lead you to other Christians with whom you can have fellowship. Ask Him to direct you to a fellowship or group of believers which will best fit your needs and enable you to grow in knowledge of Him. He is faithful, and He will do it.

What are angels?

The word "angel" or "angels" appears 386 times in the Bible so I believe we can assume that it is important to understand what they are and what they do.

The Hebrew word *mal-awk'* and the Greek word *ang'-el-os* translated as "angel" both mean "messenger". It is used to refer to an ordinary messenger, such as a prophet, priest or minister of the New Testament, but it also refers to certain heavenly beings used by God to carry on the government of this world.

Jesus told the disciples that children have angels.

Take heed that ye despise not one of these little ones; for I say unto you, That in heaven their angels do always behold the face of my Father which is in heaven. (Matthew 18:10)

Most of us have heard of these "guardian angels". It doesn't specifically say here that the children's angels "guard" them precisely, but let's look at another scripture.

For he shall give his angels charge over thee, to keep thee in all thy ways. (Psalms 91:11)

We see here that God does give his angels charge over us to guard us. Well then, why does it appear that they don't always do their job?

I believe we can find the answer in this next passage.

Bless the LORD, ye his angels, that excel in strength, that do his commandments, hearkening unto the voice of his word. (Psalms 103:20)

It tells us here that the angels listen to the voice of God's Word. It is when we speak the Word of God into our lives that our angels are empowered to intervene in our behalf.

Notice this scripture only says they listen to God's Word. How do we know that they will help us?

The Bible answers this question in the following passage:

But to which of the angels said he at any time, Sit on my right hand, until I make thine enemies thy footstool?
Are they not all ministering spirits, sent forth to minister for them who shall be heirs of salvation? (Hebrews 1:13,14)

We see here that angels are "ministering spirits" sent to minister for them who are the "heirs of salvation". And who are the "heirs of salvation"? That is referring to us, believers in Christ.

And if ye be Christ's, then are ye Abraham's seed, and heirs according to the promise. (Galatians 3:29)

It is important to remember how we empower our angels to operate on our behalf:

Bless the LORD, ye his angels, that excel in strength, that do his commandments, hearkening unto the voice of his word. (Psalms 103:20)

Angels respond to the Word of God. If we want our angels to protect us and execute the will of God on our behalf, it is important to speak the Word pertaining to those circumstances to give them something on which to act.

When we are sick, we don't lay around complaining about how bad we feel, we speak what the Word says about us. What does the Word say?

Surely he hath borne our griefs [sickness], *and carried our sorrows* [pain]: *...and with his stripes <u>we are healed.</u>* (Isaiah 53:4, 5)

Bless the LORD, O my soul, and forget not all his benefits: Who forgiveth all thine iniquities; <u>who healeth all thy diseases;</u> (Psalms 103:2, 3)

And when we need money, instead of worrying and calling our friends, we pray and say what the Word says about our financial needs:

<u>But my God shall supply all your need</u> according to his riches in glory by Christ Jesus. (Philippians 4:19)

Recall we saw before that Jesus said,

For verily I say unto you, That whosoever shall say unto this mountain, Be thou removed, and be thou cast into the sea; and shall not doubt in his heart, but shall believe that those things which he saith shall come to pass; he shall have whatsoever he saith. (Mark 11:23)

Now we see how this happens. We also see why we must be very careful of what we say. Jesus said concerning our words,

But I say unto you, That every idle word that men shall speak, they shall give account thereof in the day of judgment. (Matthew 12:36)

We can see now why God will call us to give account of our words. When we have been entrusted with something so powerful it is imperative that we put to good use what we have been given. It is crucial that our words line up with the Word of God so that the angels whom God has assigned to us will be employed bringing about God's will on earth.

Having an understanding of the reality of angels will increase our faith. There is a story in the Old Testament about Elisha the prophet who was shown by God what the plans of the king of Syria were against the king of Israel. When the king of Syria learned of this, the Bible said he sent a "great host", which means hundreds of soldiers, to capture Elisha. When Elisha's servant saw this army he was afraid, but Elisha told him "Fear not, for they that are of us are more than they which are of them". (II Kings 6:13) Then he prayed and asked God to open the eyes of his servant so that he could see, and he saw that the mountain was full of the angels of God that God had sent to protect them.

And he answered, Fear not: for they that be with us are more than they that be with them.

And Elisha prayed, and said, LORD, I pray thee, open his eyes, that he may see. And the LORD opened the eyes of the young man; and he saw: and, behold, the mountain was full of horses and chariots of fire round about Elisha. (II Kings 6:13, 14)

Angels are always with us and around us, but it is up to us to determine whether they intervene on our behalf or not. By the words we speak, we determine what our angels can do. When we complain and criticize, they are powerless to help, but when we speak the Word of God in faith, they are empowered to come to our aid. This is one of the reasons why it is so important to know what the Word says about every aspect of our lives. This is also why we need to take custody of our words and speak only what the Word says concerning ourselves and those around us, particularly those we love.

Commit today to mount guard over your heart and mouth, that the words you say will empower your angels to bring the blessings of God into your life – health, prosperity, peace, and goodness in every area of your life.

What is "spiritual warfare"?

Our discussion of angelic beings would not be complete if we did not also mention evil angelic beings, or devils (also called "demons").

And the great dragon was cast out, that old serpent, called the Devil, and Satan, which deceiveth the whole world: he was cast out into the earth, and his angels were cast out with him. (Revelation 12:9)

And the devil that deceived them was cast into the lake of fire and brimstone, where the beast and the false prophet are, and shall be tormented day and night forever and ever. (Revelation 20:10)

We see here that Satan is an evil angel and there are other angels which follow him and do his bidding. We know from the first time we hear of him in Genesis where he appeared as a serpent and deceived Eve to give up her God-given citizenship in the Garden of Eden, and we see here that that is his function ever since, to deceive the children of God into disobedience.

Jesus said that as believers, we are to do the work of God, and the work of God is to believe Jesus and His Word, the result of which we will do the Word and do the works that Jesus did.

Then said they unto him, What shall we do, that we might work the works of God? Jesus answered and said unto them, "This is the work of God, that ye believe on him whom he hath sent." (John 6:29)

Believing God's Word [faith] causes us to do the works of God. Disbelieving God's Word [fear] causes us to do the work of the devil. We can judge what people believe by the works they do and the words they speak. Jesus said He came to destroy the works of the devil, and so should we.

"He that committeth sin is of the devil; for the devil sinneth from the beginning. For this purpose the Son of God was manifested, that he might destroy the works of the devil." (John 3:8)

"Verily, verily, I say unto you, He that believeth on me, the works that I do shall he do also; and greater works than these shall he do; because I go unto my Father. " (John 14:12)

So, our work is to destroy the work of the devil, but what is the work of the devil? Before Adam and Eve listened to the devil and lost their place in the Garden of Eden their life was as "heaven on earth". Even the old covenant promised "heaven on earth".

That your days may be multiplied, and the days of your children, in the land which the LORD swore unto your fathers to give them, as the days of heaven upon the earth. (Deuteronomy 11:21)

So, we can assume that anything that cannot be found in heaven is a "work of the devil". Sickness cannot be found in heaven, so sickness is a work of the devil. Poverty and lack cannot be found in heaven, so poverty and lack are works of the devil. It is patently obvious that since God is love, then hate, resentment, bitterness, greed, selfishness, and all that results from these things are works of the devil. But how do we destroy these things? It is certainly not by retaliating in like kind. Jesus commanded us to love our enemies, not just our friends.

But I say unto you, Love your enemies, bless them that curse you, do good to them that hate you, and pray for them which despitefully use you, and persecute you; (Mathew 5:44)

Many become confused when they see the Bible tells us to "fight the good fight of faith", thinking we must confront people constantly and return fire with fire so to speak. Many people spend most of their lives watching what the devil is doing on the earth and writing letters or picketing or organizing. But the Bible tells us that we have mightier weapons than this.

For though we walk in the flesh, we do not war after the flesh:
(For the weapons of our warfare are not carnal, but mighty through God to the pulling down of strongholds;)
Casting down imaginations, and every high thing that exalteth itself against the knowledge of God, and bringing into captivity every thought to the obedience of Christ; (II Corinthians 10:3-5)

Notice it says hear the "weapons of our warfare are not carnal". What this means is that we do not war with outward circumstances and acts. We war in the spirit. [Hence the term "spiritual warfare"] We pray.

You think this sounds sort of wimpy and somewhat of a cop-out, but just listen. Several months ago, a pornographic video store appeared in our neighborhood. I didn't write letters to the county, I didn't picket the store; I didn't even approach the manager. I never set foot in the store. What I did was pray. I cursed the finances of the store in the Name of Jesus. [You can only do this when a person is behaving illegally according to God's law. You cannot curse the finances of a Godly man or a Godly endeavor.] Within several weeks, the store was gone.

What we have to remember is that every person is either following God or following some devil. We have authority over devils.

Behold, I give unto you power to tread on serpents and scorpions, and over all the power of the enemy: and nothing shall by any means hurt you. (Luke 10:19)

"Snakes" and "scorpions" are synonyms for "devils and demons". He is saying He has given us power over devils and demons and over all the power of the enemy. When other people choose to obey evil spirits we cannot overcome their choice, this is witchcraft to overpower another person's free will. But when they choose to bring their wickedness into our territory, then we have the authority to push them back. When the pornography came into my neighborhood I had the authority to resist it in the Name of Jesus. I also prayed that the people responsible for the business would be delivered from deception and that God would send people to witness to them the saving knowledge of Christ in a way which they could receive and be set free.

As you begin to read the Word and find your place in Christ, you begin to look around you and recognize more and more what the devil is doing in the people around you, in your area, and in your country. There are times when God may lead you to do something in the natural, but most of the time, He just calls us to pray. Do not be deceived into thinking that this is not accomplishing anything. Prayer is the most powerful thing you can do. We have the power to pray that the lies of the devil be exposed and that God will send witnesses to people that they will be able to receive from, that they might believe the truth of the gospel of Christ and be set free. Jesus commanded us to pray this way.

Therefore said he unto them, "The harvest truly is great, but the laborers are few: pray ye therefore the Lord of the harvest, that he would send forth laborers into his harvest." (Luke 10:2)

God told Israel in the days of King Solomon:

"If my people, which are called by my name, shall humble themselves, and pray, and seek my face, and turn from their wicked ways; then will I hear from heaven, and will forgive their sin, and will heal their land." (Chronicles 7:14)

There are many people actively and openly engaged in trying to stem the tide of the evil that has been steadily coming in our nation. We must be good stewards of the liberties which God has given and we must be obedient to whatever God calls us to do in the natural, and sometimes He will call us to respond by natural means. But what He has called us all to do is pray. And if we don't pray, nothing we do in the natural will have any positive effect.

The book of Jude is a little book, only one chapter, but it has one of the most powerful messages in the scripture on the subject of spiritual warfare.

Beloved, when I gave all diligence to write unto you of the common salvation, it was needful for me to write unto you, and exhort you that ye should earnestly contend for the faith which was once delivered unto the saints.

For there are certain men crept in unawares, who were before of old ordained to this condemnation, ungodly men, turning the grace of our God into lasciviousness, and denying the only Lord God, and our Lord Jesus Christ. ... Likewise also these filthy dreamers defile the flesh, despise dominion, and speak evil of dignities... But these speak evil of those things which they know not: but what they know naturally, as brute beasts, in those things they corrupt themselves... These are murmurers, complainers, walking after their own lusts; and their mouth speaketh great swelling words, having men's persons in admiration because of advantage. (Jude 1:3,4,8)*

This sounds as if it was written for us today. *"These are murmurers, complainers, walking after their own lusts; and their mouth speaketh great swelling words, having men's persons in admiration because of advantage. "*

How many people today murmur and complain, seeking only to satisfy their own desires, and flattering others merely to gain advantage, rather than walking in love and deferring to others as we are commanded to do.

Jude exhorts us to "earnestly contend for the faith" which has been subverted by ungodly men (and women). To contend means to fight. But he then goes on to tell us *how* to fight.

But ye, beloved, building up yourselves on your most holy faith, praying in the Holy Ghost,
Keep yourselves in the love of God, (Jude 1:20, 21)

We fight evil by building up ourselves in faith, <u>praying in the Holy Ghost</u>.

Praying in the Holy Ghost, or praying in tongues is the single most powerful thing we can do. Recall, the verse previously that said, "The weapons of our warfare … are <u>mighty through God</u>". As we pray in the Holy Ghost, God prays His plan through us, and recall His purpose in us is to "destroy all the works of the devil". As God speaks His plan through us it becomes manifest. Recall, whatever God speaks is.

Once we are built up on our most holy faith by praying in the Holy Ghost, and keeping ourselves in the love of God, we can then approach others. Jude tells us how.

In addition, of some have compassion, making a difference.
And others save with fear, pulling them out of the fire; hating even the garment spotted by the flesh.
(Jude 1:22, 23)

By having compassion, making a difference, and above all, keeping ourselves in the love of God.

What is fasting?

To fast is to go without food. There are many references to fasting in the scripture.

*Speak unto all the people of the land, and to the priests, saying, When ye fasted and mourned in the fifth and seventh month, even those seventy years, did ye at all **fast** unto me, even to me?* (Zechariah 7:5)

*Thus saith the LORD of hosts; The **fast** of the fourth month, and the fast of the fifth, and the **fast** of the seventh, and the **fast** of the tenth, shall be to the house of Judah joy and gladness, and cheerful feasts; therefore love the truth and peace.* (Zechariah 8:19)

From these scriptures, it is clear that the people were fasting to draw near to God. There are instances in scripture where people fasted to receive favor or answers to prayer. The following passage is referring to King David who was told by the prophet Nathan that his son would die because of his [David's] sin.

The story goes that David was on his roof and saw Uriah's wife Bathsheba bathing and lusted for her and sent his servant to get her. He then sent Uriah to the front of the battle where he would be sure to be killed [which he was]. (II Samuel 11) The child who was born to them as a result of this sin was dying as God had told David through the prophet would happen.
(II Samuel 12-13)

David therefore besought God for the child; and David

*fasted, and went in, and lay all night upon the earth.
… (II Samuel 12:16)*

But despite David's fasting and praying, the child died.

*Then said his servants unto him, What thing is this that
thou hast done? thou didst **fast** and weep for the
child, while it was alive; but when the child was
dead, thou didst rise and eat bread.*
*And he said, While the child was yet alive, I fasted and
wept: for I said, Who can tell whether GOD will be
gracious to me, that the child may live?*
*But now he is dead, wherefore should I **fast**? can I
bring him back again? I shall go to him, but he
shall not return to me. (II Samuel 12:14-16,21-23)*

It is clear from these passages that David fasted in order
to facilitate his prayers.

The following passage tells of an incident when
Jehoshaphat, King of Judah fasted to empower his
prayers. He received word that a great army was
coming to attack him and he proclaimed a fast
throughout all Judah.

*Then there came some that told Jehoshaphat, saying,
There cometh a great multitude against thee from
beyond the sea on this side Syria; and, behold, they
be in Hazazon-tamar, which is En-gedi.*
*And Jehoshaphat feared, and set himself to seek the
LORD, and proclaimed a **fast** throughout all
Judah. (II Chronicles 20:3)*

Another purpose for fasting is to seek guidance from

the Lord, as we see in the following passage.

*As they ministered to the Lord, and **fasted**, the Holy Ghost said, Separate me Barnabas and Saul for the work whereunto I have called them.* (Acts 13:2)

The most common reason for fasting is for spiritual power as we see in the following example. This incident takes place after Jesus was baptized by John the Baptist.

Then was Jesus led up of the spirit into the wilderness to be tempted of the devil.
*And when he had **fasted** forty days and forty nights, he was afterward hungry.* (Matthew 4:2)

We see that Jesus fasted forty days and forty nights. The first result of this was that even though he was hungry [and we can imagine he was very hungry indeed!] He had the power to resist the temptation of the devil three times.

And when the tempter came to him, he said, If thou be the Son of God, command that these stones be made bread.
But he answered and said, "It is written, Man shall not live by bread alone, but by every word that proceedeth out of the mouth of God."
Then the devil taketh him up into the holy city, and setteth him on a pinnacle of the temple,
And saith unto him, If thou be the Son of God, cast thyself down: for it is written, He shall give his angels charge concerning thee: and in their hands they shall bear thee up, lest at any time thou dash thy foot against a stone.

Jesus said unto him, "It is written again, Thou shalt not tempt the Lord thy God."

Again, the devil taketh him up into an exceeding high mountain, and showeth him all the kingdoms of the world, and the glory of them;

And saith unto him, All these things will I give thee, if thou wilt fall down and worship me.

Then saith Jesus unto him, "Get thee hence, Satan: for it is written, Thou shalt worship the Lord thy God, and him only shalt thou serve."

Then the devil leaveth him, and, behold, angels came and ministered unto him. (Matthew 4:3-11)

We see the devil tempted Jesus three times and that Jesus resisted Him with the scriptures. In order to understand the strength of will that it took Jesus to resist this temptation you must realize that he left His power behind when he came to earth as a man. In order to become our substitute for sin it was necessary to experience our weakness completely. This passage refers to Jesus:

For we have not a high priest which cannot be touched with the feeling of our infirmities; but was in all points tempted like as we are, yet without sin. (Hebrews 4:15)

Until the Holy Spirit fell on Him as He was being baptized he lived as any other man.

And Jesus, when he was baptized, went up straightway out of the water: and, lo, the heavens were opened unto him, and he saw the Spirit of God descending like a dove, and lighting upon him: (Matthew 3:16)

It is also significant that after the Holy Spirit descended upon Jesus He did not immediately perform miracles. It was not until after this forty-day fast that Jesus began to do miracles.

There is another instance when Jesus himself told of the power of fasting. There was a child whom an evil spirit had made deaf and dumb. The child's father asked the disciples of Jesus to cast the spirit out and they could not. It is recorded that they had cast other devils out, (Luke 10:1-17) but they couldn't cast this one out.

And one of the multitude answered and said,
Master, I have brought unto thee my son, which hath a
*   dumb spirit;*
And wheresoever he taketh him, he teareth him: and he
*   foameth, and gnasheth with his teeth, and pineth*
*   away: and I spake to thy disciples that they should*
*   cast him out; and they could not...*
When Jesus saw that the people came running together,
*   he rebuked the foul spirit, saying unto him, "Thou*
*   dumb and deaf spirit, I charge thee, come out of*
*   him, and enter no more into him. "*
And the spirit cried, and rent him sore, and came out of
*   him: and he was as one dead; insomuch that many*
*   said, He is dead.*
But Jesus took him by the hand, and lifted him up; and
*   he arose.*
And when he was come into the house, his disciples
*   asked him privately, Why could not we cast him*
*   out?*
And he said unto them, "This kind can come forth by
*   nothing, but by prayer and **fasting**. "*
(Mark 9:17-29)

This boy had had a "dumb spirit", or a demon, which caused him to not be able to talk. He had had it since he was small. The disciples tried to cast it out and they could not. We read in an earlier passage where the disciples had cast out demons, but they couldn't cast out this one. Notice Jesus told them the reason they couldn't cast this devil out is because it could only be cast out by prayer and fasting.

There are several kinds of fasts. One way of fasting is to neither drink nor eat. Both Jesus and Moses fasted this way for forty days and forty nights.

*And he was there with the LORD forty days and forty nights; **he did neither eat bread, nor drink water.** And he wrote upon the tables the words of the covenant, the ten commandments.* (Exodus 34:28)

I would not recommend you do this unless you are certain you have a clear direction from the Lord to do so and have previously fasted.

When Queen Esther was preparing to petition the King for the lives of her people, she asked them to fast three days for her.

*Go, gather together all the Jews that are present in Shushan, and **fast** ye for me, and neither eat nor drink three days, night or day: I also and my maidens will fast likewise; and so will I go in unto the king, which is not according to the law: and if I perish, I perish.* (Esther 4:16)

Another kind of fast is to abstain from certain foods.

We read in the book of Daniel where Daniel engaged in this type of fast.

I ate no pleasant bread, neither came flesh nor wine in my mouth, neither did I anoint myself at all, till three whole weeks were fulfilled. (Daniel 10:3)

The result of this fast is very instructive. This is the result of that fast, in Daniel's own words:

Then I lifted up mine eyes, and looked, and behold a certain man clothed in linen, whose loins were girded with fine gold of Uphaz:

His body also was like the beryl, and his face as the appearance of lightning, and his eyes as lamps of fire, and his arms and his feet like in color to polished brass, and the voice of his words like the voice of a multitude... Then said he unto me, Fear not, Daniel: for from the first day that thou didst set thine heart to understand, and to chasten thyself before thy God, thy words were heard, and I am come for thy words.

But the prince of the kingdom of Persia withstood me one and twenty days: but, lo, Michael, one of the chief princes, came to help me; and I remained there with the kings of Persia. (Daniel 10:5,6,12,13)

The result of this fast was that an angel came to Daniel's aid. Do you need an angel to help you? Try fasting and praying.

Notice that the angel told Daniel that he was sent the first day that Daniel began to pray but it took twenty-one days to reach him because he was hindered by demonic opposition. We again see illustrated the power of fasting to overcome demonic opposition.

Finally, this scripture outlines the manifold benefits of fasting:

*Is not this the **fast** that I have chosen? to loose the bands of wickedness, to undo the heavy burdens, and to let the oppressed go free, and that ye break every yoke?*

Is it not to deal thy bread to the hungry, and that thou bring the poor that are cast out to thy house? when thou seest the naked, that thou cover him; and that thou hide not thyself from thine own flesh?

Then shall thy light break forth as the morning, and thine health shall spring forth speedily: and thy righteousness shall go before thee; the glory of the LORD shall be thy rearward.

Then shalt thou call, and the LORD shall answer; thou shalt cry, and he shall say, Here I am. If thou take away from the midst of thee the yoke, the putting forth of the finger, and speaking vanity;

And if thou draw out thy soul to the hungry, and satisfy the afflicted soul; then shall thy light rise in obscurity, and thy darkness be as the noonday:

And the LORD shall guide thee continually, and satisfy thy soul in drought, and make fat thy bones: and thou shalt be like a watered garden, and like a spring of water, whose waters fail not. (Isaiah 59:6,11)

This tells us that fasting will undo heavy burdens so that the oppressed can go free, it will bring healing, it will help us to walk in righteousness, it will bring protection, it will bring fullness to our soul and we will be satisfied even when the rest of the world is hungry.

When I first became a Christian, I was hungry for all of God that I could get. When I first learned about fasting I used to fast every Thursday until 5:00PM drinking only liquids and not eating. I found it magnified my awareness of the presence of God in my life. I have since found that when my awareness of Him grows faint, fasting is a very powerful way of drawing near to Him again. I believe this was what Jesus was referring to in the following passage.

*Then came to him the disciples of John, saying, Why do we and the Pharisees **fast** oft, but thy disciples **fast** not?*

*And Jesus said unto them, Can the children of the bridechamber mourn, as long as the bridegroom is with them? but the days will come, when the bridegroom shall be taken from them, and then shall they **fast.***

No man putteth a piece of new cloth unto an old garment, for that which is put in to fill it up taketh from the garment, and the rent is made worse.

Neither do men put new wine into old bottles: else the bottles break, and the wine runneth out, and the bottles perish: but they put new wine into new bottles, and both are preserved. (Matthew 9:14-17)

Jesus says we cannot put new wine into old bottles or else the bottles will break. He tells this parable in connection with what he is saying about fasting. I believe what He is saying here is that when we fast we bring the body under subjection. Our body is the container for our soul. The Holy Spirit is often referred to as "new wine". Fasting helps to make us better vessels to contain the Holy Spirit and allow Him to work through us. As a Christian we are commanded to "walk in the spirit" in order to not fulfill the "lusts of the flesh". We are to be ruled by our spirits, rather than by our bodies and fleshly desires. According to this passage in Matthew, fasting empowers us to do just that.

To summarize the benefits of fasting are manifold. It draws us nearer to God, it empowers our prayers, it enables us to overcome demonic opposition to our prayers, and it enables us to be led by the more strongly led by the Holy Spirit. It is clearly one of the most powerful tools available to us in our Christian walk.

What is tithing?

The word "tithe" means one-tenth. The first mention of tithing is in the book of Leviticus.

And all the tithe of the land, whether of the seed of the land, or of the fruit of the tree, is the LORD's: it is holy unto the LORD.

And concerning the tithe of the herd, or of the flock, even of whatsoever passeth under the rod, the tenth shall be holy unto the LORD. (Leviticus 27:30,32)

Notice it says a tenth of the land, and everything on the land, belongs to God. In Deuteronomy, we are told what to do with the tithe.

Thou shalt truly tithe all the increase of thy seed, that the field bringeth forth year by year.

And thou shalt eat before the LORD thy God, in the place which he shall choose to place his name there, the tithe of thy corn, of thy wine, and of thine oil, and the firstlings of thy herds and of thy flocks; that thou mayest learn to fear the LORD thy God always.

And if the way be too long for thee, so that thou art not able to carry it; or if the place be too far from thee, which the LORD thy God shall choose to set his name there, when the LORD thy God hath blessed thee:

Then shalt thou turn it into money, and bind up the money in thine hand, and shalt go unto the place which the LORD thy God shall choose:

And thou shalt bestow that money for whatsoever thy

soul lusteth after, for oxen, or for sheep, or for
wine, or for strong drink, or for whatsoever thy
soul desireth: and thou shalt eat there before the
LORD thy God, and thou shalt rejoice, thou, and
thine household,

And the Levite that is within thy gates; thou shalt not
forsake him; for he hath no part nor inheritance
with thee.

At the end of three years thou shalt bring forth all the
tithe of thine increase the same year, and shalt lay
it up within thy gates:

And the Levite, (because he hath no part nor
inheritance with thee,) and the stranger, and the
fatherless, and the widow, which are within thy
gates, shall come, and shall eat and be satisfied;
that the LORD thy God may bless thee in all the
work of thine hand which thou doest.
(Deuteronomy 14:22-29)

Notice the use to which God instructed them to put the
tithe.   They were to feast before the Lord in
thankfulness for their increase and they were to share
with the Levites (priests) and the strangers (the poor)
who had no inheritance in Israel.

This was before the temple was built. After the temple
was built, the people were commanded to bring the tithe
to the temple.

And the priest the son of Aaron shall be with the
Levites, when the Levites take tithes: and the
Levites shall bring up the tithe of the tithes unto the
house of our God, to the chambers, into the
treasure house. (Nehemiah 10:38)

As we pointed out earlier, the "tithe" or one tenth of our increase belongs to God. You may think it is selfish of God to demand one tenth of all our increase, but the truth is that everything God demands of us is for our benefit. The following passage bears this out.

Will a man rob God? Yet ye have robbed me. But ye say, Wherein have we robbed thee? In tithes and offerings.

Ye are cursed with a curse: for ye have robbed me, even this whole nation.

Bring ye all the tithes into the storehouse, that there may be meat in mine house, and prove me now herewith, saith the LORD of hosts, if I will not open you the windows of heaven, and pour you out a blessing, that there shall not be room enough to receive it.

And I will rebuke the devourer for your sakes, and he shall not destroy the fruits of your ground; neither shall your vine cast her fruit before the time in the field, saith the LORD of hosts.

And all nations shall call you blessed: for ye shall be a delightful land, saith the LORD of hosts.
(Malachi 3:8-12)

God is telling them that they have robbed Him by not bringing Him their tithes and offerings, but that if they do He will open the windows of Heaven and pour out a blessing so big that they will not have room to contain it. He promises that He will rebuke the "devourer" for their sakes that their crops and herds will not be destroyed, and that all nations will call them blessed. Not a bad return for only one tenth!

This is the old covenant law regarding tithing. Let's look at the new covenant view of tithing.

And here men that die receive tithes; but there he receiveth them, of whom it is witnessed that he liveth. (Hebrews 7:8)

In this passage, the "he" is referring to Jesus. The Holy Spirit is telling us here through Paul that even though we pay tithes to men, Jesus receives them in Heaven.

Jesus said, concerning giving:

Give, and it shall be given unto you, good measure, pressed down, and shaken together, and running over, shall men give into your bosom. For with the same measure that ye mete withal it shall be measured to you again. (Luke 6:38)

There is a spiritual law concerning giving. It is often referred to the "law of sowing and reaping". This law is being illustrated by this verse in Luke, and in the following passage.

Therefore I thought it necessary to exhort the brethren, that they would go before unto you, and make up beforehand your bounty, whereof ye had notice before, that the same might be ready, as a matter of bounty, and not as of covetousness.

But this I say, He which soweth sparingly shall reap also sparingly; and he which soweth bountifully shall reap also bountifully.

Every man according as he purposeth in his heart, so let him give; not grudgingly, or of necessity: for

God loveth a cheerful giver.
And God is able to make all grace abound toward you;
that ye, always having all sufficiency in all things,
may abound to every good work:
(As it is written, He hath dispersed abroad; he hath
given to the poor: his righteousness remaineth
forever.
Now he that ministereth seed to the sower both minister
bread for your food, and multiply your seed sown,
and increase the fruits of your righteousness;)
Being enriched in every thing to all bountifulness,
which causeth through us thanksgiving to God.
(II Corinthians 9:5-11)

Notice that the amount we reap depends on the amount we sow, if we sow bountifully, we reap bountifully, but if we sow sparingly, we reap sparingly. Notice it also says God will "multiply" your seed sown. The money you sow into the kingdom of God will be multiplied back to you. This is why God commands us to give. This is the method by He uses to increase what you have. The first ten percent of your increase is your seed. A farmer doesn't eat his seed. He knows if he does, he will have no crop the next year. The same is true of us. If we do not sow, God has nothing to multiply back to us. Zero times anything is zero. Tithing is just good sense. More importantly, this is one of the ways we can show our gratitude to our Heavenly Father for his abundant provision, and isn't it just like God that the more we show our gratitude, the more abundant His provision becomes. Always remember, you cannot outgive God.

What are the requirements of answered prayer?

Many people pray and don't really seem to obtain any results. Many people don't even expect to receive answers. On the other hand, some people seem to no sooner pray than they have answers. What is the difference? The difference is faith. We talked about faith in Chapter 5 but it is so important I would like to reiterate.

Essentially, faith is believing that the Word of God is true. The Bible tells us that whoever wants to please God must believe that He exists, and that He answers prayer.

But without faith it is impossible to please him: for he that cometh to God must believe that he is, and that he is a rewarder of them that diligently seek him. (Hebrews 11:6)

If we believe that He is a rewarder of them that diligently seek Him, then we believe that He answers prayer. Prayer is diligently seeking, and if He rewards it, then He answers. We must believe that He does.

Recall, Jesus put it this way:

Therefore I say unto you, What things soever ye desire, when ye pray, believe that ye receive them, *and ye shall have* them. (Mark 11:24)

Notice He said, "When you pray believe that you

receive". We must first *believe that we receive* when we pray. This is praying in faith. When we pray *hoping* we will receive, but not really sure, this isn't faith. This is hope, and a very feeble hope at that. No, Jesus said, "believe that you receive". Believe that you receive when? When you pray. This is very crucial. If we believe we receive when we pray, once we pray, we have it. It is settled. We don't need to continue to ask, we just thank him for the answer until we see it.

Jesus also said, "Whatsoever you ask the Father in my name I will do it"

And whatsoever ye shall ask in my name, that will I do, that the Father may be glorified in the Son.
If ye shall ask any thing in my name, I will do it.
(John 14:13,14)

If we believe that Jesus means what He said, then we will believe that when we ask the Father anything in Jesus' Name He will do it. So, as soon as we pray, we can count it done. That means we receive it when we pray.
If your child asks you to pick him up from school and you tell him you will, do you expect him to be waiting for you when you get there, or do you expect him not to believe you and just take the bus anyway. No, you expect him to be counting on you to come. But this is what we do to our Heavenly Father. We ask Him to come get us, and then we just take the bus and then we wonder why He didn't come.

The first condition to answered prayer is to *believe that you receive.* If I believe that I received when I asked

God to make a way to pay my phone bill, I will not go around telling people that they are going to shut off my phone.

The second condition to answered prayer is you must say what you want to get.

For verily I say unto you, That whosoever shall say unto this mountain, Be thou removed, and be thou cast into the sea; and shall not doubt in his heart, but shall believe that those things which he saith shall come to pass; he shall have whatsoever he saith. (Mark 11:24)

This is Jesus speaking here. Notice he said "whosoever" will have "whatsoever" he says. "Whosoever" means you. "Whatsoever" means whatever you ask. And again, he gives believing as a condition for receiving but he puts it a little stronger here. He says "and shall not doubt in his heart". Well if you truly believe, you won't doubt, will you. But notice he uses the word "say" three times. Whosoever shall *say* ... and believe the things he *says* will have whatsoever he *says*. What we say is very important. Jesus says we have what we say. We need to say what we want to have and not something else.

Many people pray, but they don't really say what they want. They just ask God vaguely to do something. No, Jesus said you will have what you say. If you don't say anything, you probably won't get anything.

One of the most powerful scripture on how faith works is this one:

But the righteousness which is of faith speaketh on this

wise,

But what saith it? The word is nigh thee, even *in thy mouth, and in thy heart: that is, the word of faith, which we preach;* (Romans 10:6,8)

What this scripture is saying is that "faith speaks". When we truly believe what we say lines up with what we believe. But what does faith "speak"? Verse 8 tells us that what it says is what the Word says. We need to know what the Word says and speak what the Word says.

It goes on to say:

That if thou shalt confess with thy mouth the Lord Jesus, and shalt believe in thine heart that God hath raised him from the dead, thou shalt be saved.
For with the heart man believeth unto righteousness; and with the mouth confession is made unto salvation. (Romans 10:6-10)

Notice it says the heart believes unto righteousness, but the mouth "confesses" unto salvation. The Greek word *hom-ol-og-eh'-o* translated as "confess" means to "say the same thing". What are we to "say the same thing" as? Verse 8 tells us. We are to speak the Word of faith. We need to confess the Word, or say what the Word says about our situation, not what we see, think or feel.

Jesus also said this.

If ye abide in me, and my words abide in you, ye shall ask what ye will, and it shall be done unto you. (John 15:7)

Note the conditions Jesus is giving here for receiving what we ask. The first "If you abide in me". How do we "abide" in Jesus? To "abide" means to live. He tells us how to do that in the following verse.

If ye keep my commandments, ye shall abide in my love; even as I have kept my Father's commandments, and abide in his love. (John 15:10)

So to abide in Jesus we must keep His commandments. What are His commandments? He tells us here:

Jesus said unto him, "Thou shalt love the Lord thy God with all thy heart, and with all thy soul, and with all thy mind.
This is the first and great commandment.
And the second is like unto it, Thou shalt love thy neighbor as thyself.
On these two commandments hang all the law and the prophets. " (Matthew 22:37-40)

These verses make it very clear. To "abide" in Jesus means to walk in love. If we are not getting answers to prayer, we need to check our hearts and determine are we walking in love.

The Bible gives us a very clear picture of how to walk in love in I Corinthians 13.

Love is patient, love is kind. It does not envy, it does not boast, it is not proud.
It is not rude, it is not self-seeking, it is not easily angered, it keeps no record of wrongs.
Love does not delight in evil but rejoices with the truth.

It always protects, always trusts, always hopes, always
*   perseveres.*
Love never fails.
(I Corinthians 13:4-8; NIV)

The Greek language has several words for "love". The Greek word used here, *ag-ah'-pay* means unconditional love, the kind of love God has for us. The text tells us love is patient and kind. Love doesn't envy or put itself first. Love isn't proud. Love doesn't behave in a way that draws attention to itself, it doesn't seek it's own way, it isn't easily offended, and it doesn't think evil thoughts. It doesn't rejoice in sin, but it rejoices in truth. Love bears all things, believes all things, endures all things and love never fails. This is our standard by which we are to judge ourselves. Read it very carefully and decide if you are complying with this description and then ask the Holy Spirit to forgive you where you fall short and help you love others with His perfect love.

The second condition Jesus gave in John 15:10 for answered prayer is that "my words abide in you". His Word must be "abiding" or living in our hearts. Again, we see we must know His Word.

When we know what the Bible says about healing, we will have no difficulty believing for healing, because the Bible says God heals all our diseases.

Bless the LORD, O my soul, and forget not all his
*   benefits:*
Who forgiveth all thine iniquities; who healeth all thy
diseases; (Psalms 103:3)

When we know what the Bible says about prosperity, we can confidently believe for financial provision.

But my God shall supply all your need according to his riches in glory by Christ Jesus. (Philippians 4:19)

The fourth thing we need to examine regarding answered prayer is are we living in obedience to God's will. If there is unconfessed sin in our heart God will not hear our prayer.

If I regard iniquity in my heart, the Lord will not hear me: (Psalms 66:18)

Jesus has paid the price for our sins to be forgiven, but before they can be forgiven, we must acknowledge them and be committed to turning away from them.

If we confess our sins, he is faithful and just to forgive us our sins, and to cleanse us from all unrighteousness. (I John 1:9)

Jesus is faithful to forgive our sin and to enable us by the power of the Holy Spirit to lead a Holy life, but we must keep very short accounts in order to have our prayers answered. We all fall short of God's perfect will daily and we must be very diligent to take account of our actions and submit them to the examination of the Holy Spirit so that our fellowship with the Father is not hindered. Only then can we expect Him to hear us when we pray.

And if we know that he hear us, whatsoever we ask, we know that we have the petitions that we desired of him. (I John 5:15)

The Bible gives us another condition for answered prayer. Immediately after telling us that if we believe we receive the things we ask, we will have what we say, Jesus commands us to forgive. Forgiveness is crucial to answered prayer.

And when ye stand praying, forgive, if ye have aught against any: that your Father also which is in heaven may forgive you your trespasses.
But if ye do not forgive, neither will your Father which is in heaven forgive your trespasses. (Mark 11:25, 26)

Notice these last two conditions are simply obeying the commandments that Jesus gave us, on which He said, "hang all the law and the prophets". Namely, we are to love God with all our heart, soul, mind and strength, and to love our neighbor as ourselves.

Jesus said ..., "Thou shalt love the Lord thy God with all thy heart, and with all thy soul, and with all thy mind.
This is the first and great commandment.
And the second is like unto it, Thou shalt love thy neighbor as thyself.
On these two commandments hang all the law and the prophets." (Matthew 22:37- 40)

So let's review. First, we believe that God is God and that He does answer prayer. Then we examine our hearts and make sure that we are walking in love. If we have any unconfessed sin, we ask forgiveness and strength to overcome weakness in this area. If we have any unforgiveness, we make a determined decision to forgive and walk in love. We then find the promise in the Word that God desires us to have what we ask and ask in faith, doubting nothing, in full confidence that what God has promised He is able to perform. (Romans 4:21)

If we believe when we pray that we will receive what we ask, how will we act? I would hope we would be thankful and thank God. Therefore, the next step is praise. We need to praise God for the answer, and keep praising Him until we see the answer. If we believe we received when we prayed, as Jesus instructed us to in Mark 11:24, we will not keep asking, we will just keep praising until the answer comes. In the story of the fig tree in Mark 11 it took only two days, and in the example of Daniel three weeks. No matter how long it takes, remember, God is faithful.

Let us hold fast the profession of our faith without wavering; (for he is faithful that promised;)
(Hebrews 10:23)

The Greek word *hom-ol-og-ee'-ah* translated here as "profession", means "to say the same thing as". We are to continue "saying the same thing as" the Word says about our situation until God changes our situation to line up with the Word.

The last point we need to remember about prayer, and perhaps the most important comes from the following passage. This is Jesus speaking here:

Therefore I say unto you, What things soever ye desire, when ye pray, believe that ye receive them, and ye shall have them. Mark 11:24

Notice He says to believe you receive "when you stand praying". Not when you see the answer, but when you pray. In other words, once you ask, it is already done.

We continue to thank Him that what we have asked according to His Word, He will do. How do we know He will?

...For He is faithful that promised. (Hebrews 10:23)

Why do bad things happen to good people?

Many are the afflictions of the righteous: but the LORD delivereth him out of them all. (Psalms 34:19)

The Hebrew word *raw-aw'* translated as "afflictions" can also be translated as "adversity, calamity, distress, evil, misery, sorrow, trouble, or wretchedness". Pretty miserable stuff. And this scripture is telling us that all this wretchedness comes to the righteous, not just the wicked. But look at the second part of the verse "But the Lord delivers him out of them all". Out of "some of them"? No, out of them ALL.

Well then why are we not seeing all Christians delivered out of all their troubles? After all, we are the "righteousness of God in Christ".

For he hath made him to be sin for us, who knew no sin; that we might be made the righteousness of God in him.
(II Corinthians 5:21)

So why are we not always delivered out of all our troubles? I believe the answer can be found in this scripture.

My people are destroyed for lack of knowledge...
(Hosea 4:6)

This is God speaking in this passage and He is saying that His people are destroyed because of lack of knowledge. As we read on in the verse, we see that it is the knowledge of the law, or the Word, to which He refers.

My people are destroyed for lack of knowledge: because thou hast rejected knowledge, I will also reject thee, that thou shalt be no priest to me: seeing thou hast forgotten the law of thy God, I will also forget thy children. (Hosea 4:6)

This scripture is speaking of people under the old covenant, but it is still true today.

We talked in the previous chapter about how to pray the prayer of faith. We discussed the importance of knowing what the Word says about whatever it is we are praying about so that we can pray in confidence knowing what the will of God is pertaining to our need. It is the same with protection as it is with healing or provision. When we know that God has angels He can send to protect us from all harm, then we can safely pray each day for the protection of those angels over ourselves and our family and anyone else for whom God puts on our heart to intercede.

I had a friend who spent time serving in the military in Iraq during the recent occupation, and every day I would plead the Blood of Jesus over Him and thank God for angels protecting him from all harm. When he came home, he was whole in body and mind and had never even seen anything that would cause him to even have bad dreams. That is protection!

God's promises are not automatic. We must appropriate them by faith. We have seen in the previous chapters on prayer and on faith, that we do this by speaking the Word into our lives.

Begin each day by speaking the protection of God promised in the following passage:

1 *He that dwelleth in the secret place of the most High shall abide under the shadow of the Almighty.*

2 *I will say of the LORD, He is my refuge and my fortress: my God; in him will I trust.*

3 *Surely he shall deliver thee from the snare of the fowler, and from the noisome pestilence.*

4 *He shall cover thee with his feathers, and under his wings shalt thou trust: his truth shall be thy shield and buckler.*

5 *Thou shalt not be afraid for the terror by night; nor for the arrow that flieth by day;*

6 *Nor for the pestilence that walketh in darkness; nor for the destruction that wasteth at noonday.*

7 *A thousand shall fall at thy side, and ten thousand at thy right hand; but it shall not come nigh thee.*

8 *Only with thine eyes shalt thou behold and see the reward of the wicked.*

9 *Because thou hast made the LORD, which is my refuge, even the most High, thy habitation;*

10 *There shall no evil befall thee, neither shall any plague come nigh thy dwelling.*

11 *For he shall give his angels charge over thee, to keep thee in all thy ways.*

12 *They shall bear thee up in their hands, lest thou dash thy foot against a stone.*

13 *Thou shalt tread upon the lion and adder: the young lion and the dragon shalt thou trample under feet*

14 *Because he hath set his love upon me,*

therefore will I deliver him: I will set him on high, because he hath known my name.

15 He shall call upon me, and I will answer him: I will be with him in trouble; I will deliver him, and honor him.

16 With long life will I satisfy him, and show him my salvation. (Psalm 91)

This scripture contains a promise for deliverance from every evil in life that may try to come against you. It begins by saying "He that dwelleth in the secret place of the Most High". What is the secret place of the Most High? Would you say Jesus is the Most High? As Christians, the Bible tells us we are in Christ.

Now he which establisheth us <u>with you in Christ</u>, and hath anointed us, is God; (II Corinthians 1:21)

If we are in Christ, we are in the Secret Place of the Most High. It is not a secret to us, but it is a secret to those who don't know Him. And all the promises of this scripture belong to us. Read it over very carefully and meditate on it until you have it in your heart, and confess the promises in it every day.

For example, begin by saying, "I thank you Father that I dwell in your secret place, I abide under your shadow. You are my refuge and my fortress and I trust in you…" Notice it says sickness will not come near your dwelling. It says He will honor you with long life and show you His salvation. When you walk in the confidence that God has promised you long life, you will not walk in fear of having your life cut short by tragedy.

But remember, you must speak the promises of God into your life. They belong to you, but you must receive them by faith, by speaking the Word of faith into your life.

The Bible tells us "As you received Christ so walk in Him".

As ye have therefore received Christ Jesus the Lord, so walk ye in him: (Colossians 2:6)
And how did you receive Him? By believing that He is the Son of God and confessing Him as Lord.

But the righteousness which is of faith speaketh on this wise...
But what saith it? The word is nigh thee, even in thy mouth, and in thy heart: that is, the word of faith, which we preach;
That if thou shalt confess with thy mouth the Lord Jesus, and shalt believe in thine heart that God hath raised him from the dead, thou shalt be saved.
For with the heart man believeth unto righteousness; and with the mouth confession is made unto salvation. (Romans 10:6.8-10)

You believed the Word of faith concerning Christ and confessed [said the same thing as] what the Word said about Him. So you walk in Him the same way you received Him, by confessing what the Word says concerning your life. This is how you appropriate God's will for every area your life. And God's will is blessing in every area of your life - protection, health, prosperity, and peace.

What is the "second coming of Christ"?

When Jesus ascended into Heaven, the angels who appeared at that time told the disciples that He would return in the same way. This is what they said:

And while they looked steadfastly toward heaven as he went up, behold, two men stood by them in white apparel;
Which also said, Ye men of Galilee, why stand ye gazing up into heaven? this same Jesus, which is taken up from you into heaven, shall so come in like manner as ye have seen him go into heaven. (Acts 1:11)

From that time until now, Christians have been expecting His return.

There are many prophesies in the Bible pertaining to this event. I do not intend to go into a detailed account of it, I just want to mention enough so that you know to expect Him and walk daily in the light of the knowledge of His return. Many events have been prophesied to take place before His return which could not have happened until recent years. For example, Daniel prophesies concerning the end time:

But thou, O Daniel, shut up the words, and seal the book, even to the time of the end: many shall run to and fro, and knowledge shall be increased. (Daniel 12:4)

This verse is the last in a passage where God is speaking to Daniel of the end times. (Daniel 11-12)

Notice it says, "Knowledge shall be increased". Until the end of the nineteenth century, technology was much the same as it was in the time of Jesus. Since the discovery of electricity and the development of the means to harness and utilize it, technology has increased at an exponential rate. We now have the technology to monitor the movements of every person on earth. Men have walked on the moon. Notice the passage "many shall run to and fro". Until recent years, this meant on foot, on horseback, and for a privileged few, horse-drawn carriages. At the present time, there are few people in this country who do not own automobiles, most have flown in airplanes at one time or another, and we even have rockets taking people beyond the moon.

Other signs of the end are given in the following passage. The disciples were asking Jesus what would be the sign of the end of the age. (The Greek word *ahee-ohn'* translated here as "world" literally means "age" or "period of time".)

And as he sat upon the mount of Olives, the disciples came unto him privately, saying, Tell us, when shall these things be? and what shall be the sign of thy coming, and of the end of the world? (Matthew 24:3)

This is Jesus' reply:

And Jesus answered and said unto them, "Take heed that no man deceive you.
For many shall come in my name, saying, I am Christ; and shall deceive many.
And ye shall hear of wars and rumors of wars: see that

*ye be not troubled: for all these things must come
to pass, but the end is not yet.*

*For nation shall rise against nation, and kingdom
against kingdom: and there shall be famines, and
pestilences, and earthquakes, in divers places.*

All these are the beginning of sorrows.

*Then shall they deliver you up to be afflicted, and shall
kill you: and ye shall be hated of all nations for my
name's sake.*

*And then shall many be offended, and shall betray one
another, and shall hate one another.*

*And many false prophets shall rise, and shall deceive
many.*

*And because iniquity shall abound, the love of many
shall wax cold.*

*But he that shall endure unto the end, the same shall be
saved.*

*And this gospel of the kingdom shall be preached in all
the world for a witness unto all nations; and then
shall the end come.* (Matthew 24:4 - 14)

Notice the last verse:

*And this gospel of the kingdom shall be preached in all
the world for a witness unto all nations; and then
shall the end come.*

Only in the last century has it become possible for the
gospel to be preached to **all nations.** In the times
before technology, when travel was limited to horses,
horse drawn vehicles and foot, it would have been
virtually impossible for the entire planet to receive the
gospel in any one generation. But with today's
technology, this is not only possible, it is rapidly being

accomplished.

Jesus goes on to tell us:

For then shall be great tribulation, such as was not since the beginning of the world to this time, no, nor ever shall be.

And except those days should be shortened, there should no flesh be saved: but for the elect's sake those days shall be shortened.

Then if any man shall say unto you, Lo, here is Christ, or there; believe it not.

For there shall arise false Christs, and false prophets, and shall show great signs and wonders; insomuch that, if it were possible, they shall deceive the very elect.

Behold, I have told you before.

Wherefore if they shall say unto you, Behold, he is in the desert; go not forth: behold, he is in the secret chambers; believe it not.

For as the lightning cometh out of the east, and shineth even unto the west; so shall also the coming of the Son of man be. (Matthew 24:21 - 27)

You need to take note of this passage. It says if any one should tell you Jesus is here, you are not to believe it, because when Jesus comes it will be like the lightning coming from the east to the west. Everyone will know; you won't have to be told.

Immediately after the tribulation of those days shall the sun be darkened, and the moon shall not give her light, and the stars shall fall from heaven, and the powers of the heavens shall be shaken:

And then shall appear the sign of the Son of man in heaven: and then shall all the tribes of the earth mourn, and they shall see the Son of man coming in the clouds of heaven with power and great glory.

And he shall send his angels with a great sound of a trumpet, and they shall gather together his elect from the four winds, from one end of heaven to the other.

Now learn a parable of the fig tree; When his branch is yet tender, and putteth forth leaves, ye know that summer is nigh:

So likewise ye, when ye shall see all these things, know that it is near, even at the doors.

Verily I say unto you, This generation shall not pass, till all these things be fulfilled. (Matthew 24:29 – 34)

The important thing to note in the previous verses is that as we know summer is near, so should we be aware that the return of the Lord is near. Bible scholars believe that the fig tree is symbolic of Israel, and the "putting forth leaves" refers to Israel becoming a nation. This happened in 1948, although they didn't totally recover all the land that is today Israel until 1967. In Biblical terms a "generation' is 40 years. By this reasoning, the return of the Lord should be soon. We need to live as if we are constantly expecting His return in any case.

Therefore be ye also ready: for in such an hour as ye think not the Son of man cometh. (Matthew 24:44)

Let's look again at the following verses:

And ye shall hear of wars and rumors of wars: see that
ye be not troubled: for all these things must come
to pass, but the end is not yet.
For nation shall rise against nation, and kingdom
against kingdom: and there shall be famines, and
pestilences, and earthquakes, in divers places.
All these are the beginning of sorrows.
(Matthew 24:6-8)

The Greek word *o-deen'* translated as "sorrows" means literally "birth pangs". There have been wars, earthquakes, famines and pestilences for many centuries, but it is not until recently that the occurrence of these things has escalated at such an increasing rate. Just as birth pains escalate in frequency and intensity at an increasing rate as the birth approaches, so does the escalation of the frequency and intensity of these events signify the approaching coming of the Lord.

It is important to note, however, that the entire discussion Jesus gives in Matthew 31:4-51 is referring to not one event, but two. Notice in the following verses Jesus is talking of a period in time after certain events have taken place.

And then shall appear the sign of the Son of man in
heaven: and then shall all the tribes of the earth
mourn, and they shall see the Son of man coming in
the clouds of heaven with power and great glory.
And he shall send his angels with a great sound of a
trumpet, and they shall gather together his elect
from the four winds, from one end of heaven to
the other. (Matthew 24:30, 31)

The Greek word *ek-lek-tos'* translated as "elect" means literally "chosen". He is speaking the Church of here.

It is significant that He says the angels will gather them "from one end of heaven to the other". Why is He not gathering them from the earth? Many Bible scholars believe that it is because the Church will already be in Heaven.

Before Jesus returns to bodily set foot on the earth the Church will have been gathered to Him in the air. There are several passages of scripture that speak of this event.

Behold, I show you a mystery; We shall not all sleep, but we shall all be changed,
In a moment, in the twinkling of an eye, at the last trump: for the trumpet shall sound, and the dead shall be raised incorruptible, and we shall be changed.
(I Corinthians 15:51,52)

The Greek word *koy-mah'-o* translated as "sleep" was used figuratively to mean "decease" or "die". The apostle Paul is saying that there will be a generation that will not die, but will be changed from their mortal bodies to their immortal bodies in an instant at the same time that those who have died receive their immortal physical bodies.

For this we say unto you by the word of the Lord, that we which are alive and remain unto the coming of the Lord shall not prevent them which are asleep.
For the Lord himself shall descend from heaven with a

shout, with the voice of the archangel, and with the
trump of God: and the dead in Christ shall rise
first:
Then we which are alive and remain shall be caught up
together with them in the clouds to meet the Lord in
the air: and so shall we ever be with the Lord.
Wherefore comfort one another with these words.
(I Thessalonians 4:15-18)

He is saying that with the trump [trumpet] of God, first the dead in Christ will be resurrected in their new bodies, and those are alive and remain on earth until that time will be changed and caught up together with them in the air. This event must precede the "Second Coming" when Jesus literally sets foot on earth, because Matthew 13:31 tells us that as He comes His angels gather His Church from the "one end of Heaven to the other", because when He comes bodily to earth, all the Church will be with Him.

... and the LORD my God shall come, and all the saints
with thee. (Zechariah 14:5)

In another passage when He is talking about the trouble or "tribulation" which will come on the earth He tells us,

And when these things begin to come to pass, then look
up, and lift up your heads; for your redemption draweth
nigh. (Luke 21:28)

We need to be expecting His return constantly and living lives fit for His kingdom. We need to be "about our Father's business" working for His kingdom so that when He comes we will not be ashamed, and so that we will have a reward for our labors.

Do not get discouraged because so few people are expecting His return. Notice the Bible predicts that.

Knowing this first, that there shall come in the last days
  scoffers, walking after their own lusts,
And saying, Where is the promise of his coming? for
  since the fathers fell asleep, all things continue as
  they were from the beginning of the creation. (II
  Peter 3:3,4)

Human nature has not changed. Jesus warned us that it would be now even as it was in the days of Noah, people will scoff at the Word of God.

But as the days of Noah were, so shall also the coming
  of the Son of man be. drinking, marrying and
  giving in marriage, until the day that Noah entered
  into the ark,
And knew not until the flood came, and took them all
  away; so shall also the coming of the Son of man
  be. (Matthew 13:37-39)

In the days of Noah, the people just went about their business until Noah entered the ark and the flood came. Notice God took Noah and his family out before destruction came on the earth. He will do the same for His Church.

Another passage which points to the Church being taken out before the ultimate end of violence on the earth is the following passage which immediately follows a discussion of end time events:

And take heed to yourselves, lest at any time your
hearts be overcharged with surfeiting, and
drunkenness, and cares of this life, and so that day
come upon you unawares.
For as a snare shall it come on all them that dwell on
the face of the whole earth.
Watch ye therefore, and pray always, that ye may be
accounted worthy to escape all these things that
shall come to pass, and to stand before the Son of
man. (Luke 21:34-36)

Notice He says pray that you may be "accounted worthy to escape all these things that shall come to pass, and to stand before the Son of Man".

This is another picture of being taken out of the earth to be with Jesus. This event is commonly referred to as the "Rapture of the Church". The word "rapture" comes from a Greek word *ar-padz-o* meaning "to seize" which is not actually found in scripture but is descriptive of the Church being "caught away". The term "Second Coming" is used to refer to the bodily return of Jesus to the earth with His Church.

No discussion of "end time" events would be complete without mention of the Book of Revelation. This book was written by the Apostle John who was living in exile on the island of Patmos off the coast of Greece. Jesus appeared to him in a vision and the Book of Revelation is an account of what Jesus showed him in that vision. It is an account of end time events. You should read it carefully as it describes events which will take place on the earth immediately prior to the return of Jesus. We will now look only at the following passage.

And they sung a new song, saying, Thou art worthy to take the book, and to open the seals thereof: for thou wast slain, and hast redeemed us to God by thy blood out of every kindred, and tongue, and people, and nation;

And hast made us unto our God kings and priests: and we shall reign on the earth.

And I beheld, and I heard the voice of many angels round about the throne and the beasts and the elders: and the number of them was ten thousand times ten thousand, and thousands of thousands;

Saying with a loud voice, Worthy is the Lamb that was slain to receive power, and riches, and wisdom, and strength, and honor, and glory, and blessing.

And every creature which is in heaven, and on the earth, and under the earth, and such as are in the sea, and all that are in them, heard I saying, Blessing, and honor, and glory, and power, be unto him that sitteth upon the throne, and unto the Lamb forever and ever. (Revelation 5:9-13)

This passage speaks of people "redeemed out of every kindred, and tongue and people and nation" and "every creature which is in heaven and on the earth and under the earth and such as are in the sea" appearing before the throne of God. Many Bible scholars believe that the Book of Revelation foretells events in chronological order and that the event described in this passage precedes other cataclysmic events on the earth described in the following passages. It appears from this reasoning that the Church is in Heaven with Christ before these other events occur. The time of "trouble" on the earth immediately preceding Christ's return is referred to as the "tribulation". It is indicated that there will be an evil world ruler emerge, referred to as the "anti-Christ", and that there will be a totalitarian world government which will persecute Christians. We can already see the storm clouds forming on the horizon.

Another passage that points to the soon return of Jesus can be found here:

And this gospel of the kingdom shall be preached in all the world for a witness unto all nations; and then shall the end come. (Matthew 24:14)

Jesus is speaking in this passage and he is indicating that the last thing that must be accomplished before His return is that the "gospel of the kingdom shall be preached in all the world for a witness unto all nations". Only in the last several decades has this been physically possible, but with the advent of satellite communication, the Internet and air travel, it is finally not only a possibility, but it is rapidly being accomplished. Once the Gospel has been preached to all nations, Jesus tells us "and then the end shall come. This time is rapidly approaching.

In the light of that knowledge, what should our focus be as Christians? I believe the apostle Peter answers that question in the following passage.

But the day of the Lord will come as a thief in the night; in the which the heavens shall pass away with a great noise, and the elements shall melt with fervent heat, the earth also and the works that are therein shall be burned up.

Seeing then that all these things shall be dissolved, what manner of persons ought ye to be in all holy conversation and godliness,

Looking for and hasting unto the coming of the day of God, wherein the heavens being on fire shall be dissolved, and the elements shall melt with fervent heat?

Nevertheless we, according to his promise, look for new heavens and a new earth, wherein dwelleth righteousness.

Wherefore, beloved, seeing that ye look for such things, be diligent that ye may be found of him in peace, without spot, and blameless. (II Peter 3:10-14)

We are to live a holy life in godliness "without spot and blameless". Keep this in mind:

For the grace of God that bringeth salvation hath appeared to all men,

Teaching us that, denying ungodliness and worldly lusts, we should live soberly, righteously, and godly, in this present world;

Looking for that blessed hope, and the glorious appearing of the great God and our Savior Jesus Christ.
(Titus 2:11-13)

If we will "deny ungodliness and worldly lusts, living soberly, righteously, and godly in this present world", the soon coming "glorious appearing of the great God and our Savior Jesus Christ will be our "blessed hope" and will sustain is even when the world seems to be crashing down around us.

I think it is important at this point to consider the words of Jesus as he was referring to such a time as this:

Who then is a faithful and wise servant, whom his lord hath made ruler over his household, to give them meat in due season?
Blessed is that servant, whom his lord when he cometh shall find so doing.
(Matthew 24:45, 46)

We need to be "about our Father's business" so that when the Lord comes, He will find us faithful.

It is interesting to note that the first three significant events in the Church corresponded exactly with Jewish feast days.

The first was Passover. On the feast of Passover a lamb was slain as a sacrifice to protect Israel in Egypt the night before they came out, and afterwards in order to remember their deliverance.. The crucifixion of Jesus occurred on the feast of Passover. (Exodus 12:21, John 1: 29)

The next feast day mentioned is the feast of "firstfruits".
Jesus is referred to as the firstfruits.
(Leviticus 2:12, I Corinthians 15:23)

The third feast is the feast of Pentecost. This comes fifty days after passover (the word "pentocost" being derived from the Greek word meaning fifty). The Jewish festival celebrates the law being given to Moses which was written by God on tablets of stone. (Exodus

24:12) On the feast of Pentecost, when the first church was gathered in the "upper room" in Jerusalem, the Holy Spirit descended and fell on all the believers. The Holy Spirit was sent to write the law on the hearts of God's people. (Jerimiah 31:33)

The next feast day is Rosh Hashannah. This feast celebrates the beginning of the Jewish New Year. Traditionally the Rabbi's have taught that at midnight on Rosh Hashannah the eastern sky will break open and Messiah will appear. It is interesting to note that on the feast of Rosh Hashannah a shofar (trumpet made of a ram's horn) is blown. Contrast this with the following passage:

For the Lord himself shall descend from heaven with a
shout, with the voice of the archangel, and with the
trump of God: and the dead in Christ shall rise
first:
Then we which are alive and remain shall be caught up
together with them in the clouds, to meet the
Lord in the air: and so shall we ever be with the
Lord.
(I Thesselonians 4:17)

I close with the words of the apostle John:

He which testifieth these things saith,
"Surely I come quickly. Amen."
Even so, come, Lord Jesus.
The grace of our Lord Jesus Christ be with you all.
Amen. (Revelation 22:20, 21)

Made in the USA
Charleston, SC
21 December 2014